Tony Carter, PhD, JD

Many Thin Companies
The Change in Customer Dealings and Managers Since September 11, 2001

29

Many Thin Companies
The Change in Customer Dealings and Managers Since September 11, 2001

BEST BUSINESS BOOKS
Robert E. Stevens, PhD
David L. Loudon, PhD
Editors in Chief

Strategic Planning for Collegiate Athletics by Deborah A. Yow,
R. Henry Migliore, William W. Bowden, Robert E. Stevens,
and David L. Loudon

*Church Wake-Up Call: A Ministries Management Approach That
Is Purpose-Oriented and Inter-Generational in Outreach*
by William Benke and Le Etta N. Benke

Organizational Behavior by O. Jeff Harris and Sandra J. Hartman

Marketing Research: Text and Cases by Bruce Wrenn, Robert Stevens,
and David Loudon

Doing Business in Mexico: A Practical Guide by Gus Gordon
and Thurmon Williams

Employee Assistance Programs in Managed Care by Norman Winegar

*Marketing Your Business: A Guide to Developing a Strategic Marketing
Plan* by Ronald A. Nykiel

*Customer Advisory Boards: A Strategic Tool for Customer Relationship
Building* by Tony Carter

Fundamentals of Business Marketing Research by David A. Reid
and Richard E. Plank

*Many Thin Companies: The Change in Customer Dealings
and Managers Since September 11, 2001* by Tony Carter

Marketing Management: Text and Cases by David L. Loudon, Robert E.
Stevens, and Bruce Wrenn

Selling in the New World of Business by Bob Kimball and Jerold "Buck"
Hall

Many Thin Companies
The Change in Customer Dealings and Managers Since September 11, 2001

Tony Carter, PhD, JD

BEST BUSINESS BOOKS

Best Business Books®
An Imprint of The Haworth Press, Inc.
New York • London • Oxford

Published by

Best Business Books®, an imprint of The Haworth Press, Inc., 10 Alice Street, Binghamton, NY 13904-1580.

Cover design by Lora Wiggins.

Library of Congress Cataloging-in-Publication Data

Carter, Tony, 1955-
 Many thin companies : the change in customer dealings and managers since September 11, 2001 / Tony Carter.
   p. cm.
 Includes bibliographical references and index.
 ISBN 0-7890-2247-8 (hard : alk. paper)—ISBN 0-7890-2248-6 (soft : alk. paper)
 1. Industrial management—United States. 2. Business enterprises—United States. I. Title.

HD70.U5C375 2004
658.8'12—dc22

2004001794

To Walter and Calvin
my heart, soul, and inspiration

ABOUT THE AUTHOR

Tony Carter, PhD, JD, MBA, is Academic Director and Professor of Sales at the Christos M. Cotsakos College of Business in the Russ Berrie Institute for Professional Sales, William Patterson University, Wayne, New Jersey. Dr. Carter is also Adjunct Professor of Marketing at the Graduate School of Business of Columbia University, where he teaches in the MBA program. At Columbia University, he is the Associate Faculty Director of the Executive Management Programs for Sales Management and Key Account Management. In 1994-1995, he was the General Mills Visiting Professor at Columbia University.

Dr. Carter is the author of *Contemporary Sales Force Management, The Aftermath of Reengineering,* and *Customer Advisory Boards,* all from Haworth Press. In addition, he has been published in such venues as the *Harvard Business Review,* the *Columbia Journal of World Business, Business Week,* the *Journal of Professional Services Marketing,* the *Journal of Global Competitiveness, Sales and Marketing Management, Management Magazine, Selling Power,* the *Journal of Economic Literatures,* the *Journal of Personal Selling and Sales Management,* and the *Journal of Employment.* He is Editor in Chief of the *Journal of Hospital Marketing & Public Relations.*

Dr. Carter has worked as a manager for several corporations and has been a ghost lecturer at universities overseas, such as the Caucasus School of Business in Tbilisi in the Republic of Georgia. His case studies and research have been adopted and used by various universities and organizations around the world. Dr. Carter is the recipient of The *Wall Street Journal* Award and is an inductee of Delta Mu Delta—The National Honor Society in Business Administration.

CONTENTS

Foreword

Ever since the human tragedy from September 11, 2001, the world became a much tougher place to relax and organizations realized that an inevitable part of this new world condition is the ability to master change and uncertainty. In this important book, Tony Carter discusses the role of organizations and managers as a means of enriching the customer with strategies we all need to think about in today's intensely competitive world. I hope that people read this book, since it provides an arsenal of tools for lasting change, as well as lessons for enriching the quality of performance.

Dr. Joseph Stiglitz
Professor of Economics
Columbia University;
Winner of the 2001
Nobel Prize in Economics

Preface and Acknowledgments

The world changed after September 11, 2001, and this tragic event became a defining moment in history and our lives. The purpose of this book is to examine the impact of September 11 on organizations and how they operate, managers, employees and salespeople and how they perform, and customers and how they buy differently. In effect, has September 11, 2001 led to *Many Thin Companies?* The societal impact due to the loss of lives and terrorist threats to personal safety have been devastating. The business impact has been adverse as well. We know that in all areas of our lives we can never relax again. We have to be stronger and more effective in business and our own lives.

The book reviews business events since September 11, 2001, and in particular examines the airline industry and insurance industry, which were dramatically changed, consumer behavior, management practices, and the global implications of that day. I have included results from surveys with several hundred Fortune 500 and midsized companies, including Sony, Morgan Stanley/Dean Witter, J.P. Morgan Chase, Oppenheimer Corporation, GE Capital, Lubrizol, ConocoPhillips, Exxon Mobil, and the Russ Berrie Company to show how companies are facing the challenges from September 11, 2001.

I want to thank important people in my life who support and inspire what I do such as my sons Calvin and Walter, my parents, Walter Palin, Mike, Kerstein, Kirk, and Kim and Mikey. I extend many thanks to Dr. Joseph Stiglitz, the 2001 Nobel Prize winner in economics and professor at Columbia University; Dr. Berch Haroian of William Paterson University; and Jim Brown and Angelica Berrie and the staff at the Russ Berrie Institute of Professional Sales. Special thanks to my friends Everrett Surratt Charge D'Affairs of Sony Corporation; Dr. Noel Capon of the Columbia University Graduate School of Business; and Dr. Walter Rohrs. They are always impressive in everything that they do. Last, I greatly appreciate the support of my publisher over the years, The Haworth Press, and in particular Bill Cohen, Bill Palmer, and the editorial staff.

Tony Carter
Staten Island, New York

Chapter 1

Changes in Organizations and Management Practices

LEADERSHIP AND SEPTEMBER 11

In the two years after September 11, 2001, Fortune 500 firms cut 4 million jobs, about 20 percent of which were in middle-level management. Firms are now finding themselves "doing more with less."[1] Managers, employees, and salespeople have more consolidated job duties and their performance results are scrutinized more harshly. About 80 percent of Americans find their jobs and personal lives more stressful than before September 11, 2001, and there is a cost of $50 billion annually in turnover costs, lower productivity, and absenteeism.

Effective leadership is critical when the world is wrenched by a calamity of unimaginable dimensions.[2] Most of America's chief executives got to the top by following the how-to manual—business school, foreign postings, and long hours. No Harvard MBA course or corporate strategy session can prepare a chief executive to lead a corporation and thousands of employees when 110 floors come tumbling down. Since the collapse of the World Trade Center, many of the nation's chief executives registered the strange sensation of living in a world that they, always so capable, always so sure, had never encountered (see Figure 1.1).

"This is a human tragedy, not a financial tragedy," said Donald B. Marron, the chairman of UBS America.[3] "Top management ought to be highly visible," Leonard Riggio, chairman of Barnes & Noble, the largest bookstore chain in the country, said: "The only thing to think of is the awesome responsibility to 80,000 employees."[4] Many chief executives, not just the executives of businesses that had their home in the twin towers—such as Howard W. Lutnick, chief executive of Cantor Fitzgerald L. P., the bond trading firm that lost more than 700

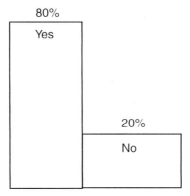

FIGURE 1.1. Organizations that have streamlined their staff and become "thinner" since September 11, 2001 (*Source:* Carter 2003.)

of its 1,000 employees, including Lutnick's brother—had to calm frayed nerves. Thousands of businesses, it turned out, had connections to the tragedy. Gap Inc., the clothing chain based in San Francisco whose khakis, denims, and colored T-shirts have little to do with the business of Wall Street, is just one example. The company had two stores in the towers—all staffers got out alive—and was forced to cope with the emergency as was everyone else.

Some corporations have had to make significant strategic changes. For example, General Electric has created a leaner, faster, more customer-focused company since September 11. The company has done this by having fewer, more efficient and higher-value jobs, and annual savings of $400 million a year in costs over the past three years. Some of this has been attributed to their using "Six Sigma," which is a statistical measure of how close a product comes to its quality goal of 99.9 percent perfect at 3.4 defects per million parts and digitalization, which is the simplification of workflow, facilitated by the Internet.[5]

For business executives schooled in focusing on the bottom line, a tragedy of this proportion upends their priorities. Profits defer to the physical and emotional well-being of their employees, the management of a business becomes the management of people in ways that are far more personal and intimate then ever before.

"You rely on your instincts, and that means people first and business is a distant second," Mr. Kim Fennebresque of SG Cowen said. "You have to ensure the physical safety of your employees and then the emotional safety of everybody." And that, Mr. Fennebresque continued, has "commercial implications." An employee who is overwrought and worried is one who cannot work. "We have to let them know that their jobs are safe, that the business is safe and they can return to work when they are ready."[6]

The late Laurence A. Tisch, former co-chairman of the Loews Corporation, a New York-based holding company of hotels, tobacco, and insurance interests, said that, for a company to move forward again, it needed to take care of the emotional needs of its employees immediately, especially in cases where there has been loss of life. "The starting place is with your own employees," Mr. Tisch said. Offer every service of condolences, he advised, and provide help for any losses within the corporate family.

> You have to make sure that those families are taken care of for life, not just for two weeks. You have to dedicate yourself to take care of the people who were hurt the least, and in that way you create the spirit to go forward. Just the fact that you have this obligation makes you go forward in the best possible way.[7]

Even such a hard-bitten Wall Streeter as John H. Gutfreund, president of Gutfreund & Company and the former chairman of Salomon Brothers, the Wall Street firm that is now part of Citigroup, sees that a tragedy will require firms—especially those that sustained major losses—to "take a fresh look" at how they run their business.

That includes where it is located, he added—outlining a rationale that, if followed by others, may spell the end of Lower Manhattan as the world's financial center.

Even though Mattel, the world's largest toy maker, is based in El Segundo, California, Robert A. Eckert, the chief executive, said he first thought of locating the company's 30,000 employees on September 11, 2001. Mr. Eckert said,

> Here at Mattel our first priority is to first assess the human safety and security. Our No. 1 priority is to find all our employees. Within an hour or two, we knew where every employee was in Mattel. We have 200 people headquartered in Manhattan and we did the head count to make sure we could find everybody. . . . And the next step goes to the question of personal leadership. . . .

he added. "You have to communicate with speed and accuracy, showing support for people. So our most important message to the people in New York City was to forget about work, worry about your families, make sure you are safe and sound.[8]

Many chief executives said that crises such as this are exactly the times for them not to retreat behind their office doors, but to be seen and heard by their employees. Communication, they say, is the key to being a leader and to assuring employees that someone is in control—especially at a time when everyone's world has suddenly become ambiguous and uncertain. That holds true, even if a company is a far-flung global empire, whose employees can be on the other side of the country or lands far away. At Mattel, e-mail is the chosen method of communication. "I have sent out an e-mail around the world once or twice a day," Mr. Eckert said.

We have 30,000 employees, the majority of whom don't even work in this country. They know directly from me what the situation is at Mattel, how we are thinking about the situation and just giving people the opportunity to know we are in control, we know what is going on and we are sympathetic.[9]

At Pfizer, the nation's largest drug maker, Dr. Henry A. McKinnell, the chief executive, was in his office when the jetliners hit the World Trade Center. With offices just one block from the United Nations and across the street from the Israeli consulate, both possible terrorist targets, Dr. McKinnell said he was very concerned about the safety of the company's employees. Immediately, he went to his office and told employees over the intercom to get away from the windows. Then he told them what he had learned about the attack from media reports.

The Thermo Electron Company, based in Waltham, Massachusetts, had eight employees in offices in the World Trade Center. Richard F. Syron, the chief executive, and the former chairman of the American Stock Exchange, said he was in the midst of preparing a memo to his employees stating that simple and grim fact that the World Trade Center had been attacked, when he got word that three had escaped and five were not there when the attack occurred.

"The first thing you do is everything you can to communicate with people about what the story is," he said.[10] Mr. Syron is now telling employees that he would never ask reluctant employees to work in what he calls "high-risk" buildings—those that are prominent and symbols of American business. Joseph Moglia, the chief executive of Ameritrade, the online broker, said one of his own children, a Merrill Lynch employee, was missing until 3 p.m. the day of the attack. However, putting that aside for a moment, following the World Trade Center attack Mr. Moglia immediately told his employees about the company's new crisis management program, which is intended to back up all existing data and retest existing systems to protect customer records.[11]

At the same time, he said that even though employees were getting much information from the media, he said he felt it was important that they be informed about what the company was doing as well. "I have always believed that the real character of a leader, of a management team, is shown in a time of crisis," Mr. Moglia said.

> We have a responsibility not only to our loved ones and employees, but to our clients. They need to know their assets are o.k. We need to be there for our clients, so they understand. In times like this, we, as leaders, need to recognize what has taken place and, at the exact same time, be supportive and understanding.[12]

During the crisis, the Walt Disney Company provided e-mail messages praising employees for the work they were doing and expressing sympathy for those in pain. One of the messages said: "I want to thank all of you—who are understandably upset, normally confused about our complicated world and tolerably angry—for being calm and calming to our guests."[13] Another, sent the day of the attacks, said: "Today's catastrophic act of violence to the World Trade Center, Pentagon, and four commercial planes is such a calamity that no words can express our shock and horror."[14]

The role of CEO is actually about being a source of emotional stability and creating an environment where people can feel safe and express how they are feeling. Virtually all of the chief executives who spoke about the disaster cited the twin executive virtues of strength and availability: strength, because people want reassurance, and availability, because they want to cry. To demonstrate strength, Mr. Marron of UBS suggested that executives visit their employees on the site of destruction if possible—though obviously not in this case. Mr. Tisch of Loews had similar counsel: "Dedicate yourself to take care of the people who were hurt or lost—and not just for two weeks—and you create the spirit to go forward."[15]

Meyer S. Frucher, chairman of the Philadelphia Stock Exchange, advises not just being available but also being physical. When the World Trade Center was bombed in 1993, Mr. Frucher was president of nearby Battery Park City and executive vice president of Olympia & York, which owned the neighboring World Financial Center. At that time, Mr. Frucher offered a triage site for victims, and Olympia and York offered free space for tenants of the World Trade Center during its rebuilding. This time, if the American Stock Exchange is unable to trade stocks in its location on Monday, the Philadelphia Stock Exchange will provide backup trading facilities as a contingency for any negative events.

Although it may seem heartless to think about rebuilding with rubble still smoldering, a chief executive who is not planning for a firm's future is a manager not worthy of his or her title, many of those interviewed for this book argued. The process of getting a firm back on its feet is therapy involving—necessity and patriotism all rolled into one.[16,17]

Roger Ailes, the chief executive of the Fox News Channel, said he would have approached the day after the debacle with a quality as a warm-blooded human being and a calculating businessperson. "You have to first assess the damage and take care of the physical and emotional needs of employees and their families," he said. "As a CEO, your job is to be a leader of people. You've got to do whatever you can to alleviate pain and damage." Mr. Ailes said that the best way to help people is to do everything possible, as quickly as possible, to get the business up and running again. "If you're going to take care of people, if you're going to pay benefits and salaries, you're going to have to have a business," he said.

> You have to operate in a way that continues to make the company function so people feel they are a part of something, so they feel they've got a home and they've got a job and they've

got something to look forward to. "You have to see what's left, where are the records, what do we have to tell shareholders and customers? Then you have to make an assessment of how many of your key people are available and put together small team of people who are functional to carry out orders.[18]

In television advertisements, Jacques A. Nasser, former chief of the Ford Motor Company, explained that he was doing his best to replace the Firestone tires said by regulators to have led to eighty-eight deaths in the United States. Masatoshi Ono of Bridgestone/Firestone does the same in full-page newspaper ads. James E. Goodwin, former chairman of United Airlines, owned by UAL, bought commercial time to offer an apology for the company's recurrent flight delays. Media analysts said they expected to see these chief executives step in front of the camera. Such appearances are now part of a chief executive's job, the analysts say.

Events of the past few years, such as President Clinton's taking to the airwaves with a personal mea culpa—have primed audiences for this strategy, said Robert J. Thompson, founder of the Center for the Study of Popular Television at Syracuse University. Now, corporate America has recognized the apology as the quickest way to make bad things go away. Putting a leader's face on a crisis response is almost a necessity now, whether for potentially fatal product flaws or annoyances such as flight delays, said Sue Parenio, an associate professor of advertising at Boston University. Americans are so intolerant with poor treatment from large corporate bureaucracies, she said, that they will accept reassurance only from the top official.

Mr. Ono, who speaks little English, did not appear in Firestone's television advertisements, which instead featured John Lampe, then executive vice president for the company's United States unit.

United Airlines had a more natural spokesman in Mr. Goodwin. On the heels of a print advertisement, United started running a TV commercial on August 24, 2002. It shows Mr. Goodwin walking through an empty airplane, presumably not one that passengers are waiting impatiently to board. It portrays him as a plain-talking, regular guy—the kind who could join a company as an accountant in 1967 and work his way up. It was shot in two hours.

Susan Fournier, an associate professor at Harvard Business School who specializes in marketing and branding, said United could take a lesson from James E. Burke, former chief of Johnson & Johnson, who saved the reputation of Tylenol during the drug-tampering scare of 1982. Mr. Burke not only appeared on numerous TV interviews, but also gave public updates on all of the company's actions, from removing products from shelves to introducing tamper-resistant packaging. "There is the acknowledgment, and then there is the reparation and recovery."[19]

Carolyn Brown, a Ford spokeswoman, said that Mr. Nasser had received good reviews for his two television advertisements. Some 58 percent of focus group members said that after watching the first ad they had a positive view of Ford's handling of the tire recall; the percentage rose to 72 for the second commercial. Reaching directly to consumers through paid advertising was an obvious choice, said Matthew Triaca, a United spokesman. Not that these executives are always willing to be their company's spokesmen. Mr. Nasser initially declined to testify at federal hearings on the tire recall, saying that others at Ford were better qualified to discuss specifics.

Still, companies are ultimately accountable for the truth in their advertisements. Americans find it hard to reject a white flag, Mr. Thompson asserted, but they are more cynical than ever. And although it is easy enough to put a human face on a company, Mr. Thompson mused, people will ask, "In the end, can a corporation really feel remorse?"

CRISIS MANAGEMENT

The occurrence of a crisis and its aftermath can have a devastating effect on a company's sales. Crisis is a major, unpredictable event that has potentially negative results.[20] Crisis management routinely deals with issues affecting the virtual survival of the corporation. Sales managers are those people in charge of the sales effort and the various functional responsibilities of the sales force, such as customer development, planning, controlling, budgeting, and decision making. They are particularly at risk when confronting a crisis, and their inability to effectively handle the crisis can change significantly the ability of the sales force to generate revenue. Accordingly, sales managers should understand the dynamics of how to prepare for and manage "worst case scenarios." Like it or not, future events will most assuredly cause harm (see Figure 1.2).

Traditionally, crisis management has been viewed negatively as "managerial fire fighting" or waiting for things to go wrong and then rushing to limit the damage. So, predicting problems not only requires a strategy to anticipate crisis situations, such as consumer protests or negative public relations. Crisis management also requires a plan of action once the crisis has occurred. For every $100 million in revenue, two incidents per year occur that call on a company's emergency response plan. For every $8 billion of revenue, there is one major loss per year, representing about one percent of annual sales. One catastrophic loss every ten years equals 1.5 times annual profit.[21] These catastrophic losses also include one or more serious injuries or deaths to employees. This is even more alarming considering that most companies do not even have a strategic system to anticipate and solve crisis situations.

Each year many more thousands of companies head down the path to failure by losing ground to competitors or watching a key piece of business disappear.[22] Sales managers must develop cultures that foster and reward the management of crisis. They must update crisis

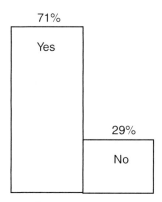

FIGURE 1.2. Companies since September 11, 2001, that have crisis management systems and planning to anticipate and solve crisis situations (*Source:* Carter 2003.)

management policies continually to ensure that they reflect changing industry dynamics.

Why do corporations fall short of objectives? Why do strategies that seemed eminently sensible turn out to be disasters? Just why do successful organizations, which once could do no wrong, suddenly begin to lose their way? Managers must fully integrate crisis management into business practices so that dealing with the crisis is not an after-the-fact exercise.

The Consequences of Crisis

Crisis can be characterized as a major unpredictable event that has potentially negative results. It can also be thought of as a turning point for better or worse. The crisis event and its aftermath may significantly change a sales organization and its salespeople, products, services, financial condition, and reputation. So, the real consequences of crisis events to sales managers can mean the loss of future sales and reputation, the loss of consumer confidence, prolonged negative publicity, exposure to lawsuits, declines in stock values, and increases in operating expenses.

Causes of Crisis

One particular cause of crisis is that senior executives too often do not understand the fundamentals of their business. They neglect to ask central questions, such as what precisely is their company's core expertise, what are reasonable long- and short-term goals, what are the key drivers of profitability in their competitive situation. It is a disturbing fact of corporate life today that many senior people at very large companies have no idea what made their organization successful.[23]

Another cause for crisis is corporate leaders who are proponents of streamlining efforts who then pump up their own bonuses while telling the troops to tighten their belts. It can be fatal to the cohesion, focus, and organization needed to respond to a crisis when cynicism and resentment build up because sales managers preach one doctrine and practice another. This brand of managerial hypocrisy goes well beyond pay and perks. Far too many sales managers ignore the human dimension of day-to-day operations, taking actions that violate unwritten rules as well as their stated intentions. They preach the importance of teamwork, then reward individuals who work at standing out from the crowd. They announce a preference for workers with broad experience then denounce job jumpers within the organization. They encourage risk taking then punish good faith failures.[24] Many future failures may take place because of the so-called new deal between workers and employers, in which traditional bonds of loyalty loosen or disappear.

Companies that offer employees a sense of long-term stability may satisfy customers and prosper at the expense of less effective competitors. Poor customer relationship building can also be a cause for crisis. About 91 percent of unhappy customers will never buy again from a company that dissatisfied them and they will communicate their displeasure to other people. Some of the various reasons that customers become dissatisfied with a company are unsatisfactory product or service quality, high price, poor location, lack of attentiveness, complacency, not having a customer complaint system, or presenting a weak public image. In addition, about one-third of all dissatisfied customers leave because they were unappreciated; some of those customers will never complain to the company. So, the failure of sales managers to have a process to monitor and meet customer satisfaction needs can be devastating to a company.

A Framework for Crisis Solutions for Sales Force Managers

Sales managers can help their organizations cope with crisis by knowing what to do before and after the crisis hits. Here are some steps to follow.

Phase One: Fact Gathering

Fact gathering is an extensive stage in the crisis management process. Certainly this is an important process to determine the best course of action when a crisis occurs. However, fact gathering should take place even before the crisis; actually it can be an ongoing process. Sales managers should determine the amount that their company spends in the region, their impact on the economy, awards and citations received, charitable donations, internal financial considerations, and the historical overview of the company. Information regarding customer dealings and, in particular, patterns of complaint by customers or regulators are important to know. All of this information from the fact-gathering process not only determines how to respond to a crisis but can have a preemptive impact with regard to those circumstances susceptible to a crisis.

Phase Two: Scenario Development

It is important for sales managers to develop the ability to anticipate and plan for crises. This can be done by forecasting and developing scenarios with the greatest probability of occurring and estimating outcomes for alternative situations. A written crisis plan should be developed that discusses these things and helps the sales department respond quickly to crisis. Also, role-playing exercises should be given to the sales force to prepare for such contingencies. These scenarios and role-plays need not distract salespeople from other sales duties and can be done during a sales meeting once or twice a year.

The main purpose of the scenario development stage of crisis management is to have a process that can identify and address all of the relevant elements of crisis readiness.

Phase Three: Communicating Our Message

This stage deals with assigning tasks and accountability and communicating this inside and outside the organization. The formation of a crisis management team is an important tool to help sales managers cope with crises. A problem with crisis management is that 43 percent of the time managers speak without authorization, 27 percent present incorrect data, and 22 percent take action that complicates the crisis. So, the crisis management team is essential to effectively communicate how the crisis is being handled. Sales managers need to either develop, or be a member of, the crisis management team.

The crisis management team should determine who is the most appropriate person to speak for the company. It should develop communication plans to inform employees, decide how to keep customers informed of events, and help establish what media will cover the crisis and who will prepare drafts of news releases and press kits. A press kit addresses external communication by dealing with all potential players and the public. The press kit also deals with internal communication by notifying the crisis team members and calling a meeting, immediately sending a memo to all employees detailing the policy, having the press monitored, and possibly even setting up an 800 number to provide easy access for questions from the public. The media plays an important role, since in many instances they dictate the existence of a crisis and determine whether it has taken place.[25]

Effective crisis management programs establish an independent unit, such as the crisis management team, to ensure objectivity and avoid vested-interest specialization. Shared responsibility allows an organization to pursue opportunities aggressively without suffering from excessive adverse exposure due to a crisis.

SYSTEM CHECKLIST

When a company has a comprehensive crisis management system, how can sales managers know it is working? Here are some clear indicators:

- Critical risk areas are identified.
- Reports are clear and concise.
- Crisis is automatically part of daily decision making.
- Crisis terminology is part of the vocabulary.
- Surprises are less frequent.
- Strategic advantages are identified.[26]

THE VISITING NURSE SERVICE OF NEW YORK AND SEPTEMBER 11

A comparison of the crisis management plans prepared before and after the World Trade Center disaster provides insight into the importance that such a plan had in the Visiting Nurse Service of New York (VNSNY). The lack of ability of management to envision an event so catastrophic is not surprising. What is hard to understand is the naiveté that is revealed in the organization's emergency and disaster plan that had been prepared in July 2000 and reviewed in July 2003.

The plan was prepared by a single individual—the director of patient services. The stated purpose involved the safety and welfare of the staff, but Human Resources was not involved in the formulation of the plan, but rather its review. No committee was appointed to gather information and/or provide insight. If an administrative-level emergency plan existed, it had not been communicated through the organization.[27]

The narrow focus for the emergency plan looked at what procedures needed to be in place to ensure continuity of patient care in the event of unusual circumstances. This included weather emergencies, interruption of essential services, and disasters, such as airplane crashes or other events that would involve significant numbers of injured or endangered persons. The VNSNY works in concert with the New York City Office of Emergency Management (OEM). In that role, VNSNY is used as a support agency. OEM conducts periodic updates, training sessions, and mock disasters. There is no agency-wide distribution of the results of these sessions, or of any changes in the existing plan that may have been warranted. In fact, the emergency and disaster plan is located in the Policy and Procedure Manual that is located in the NSNY LAN library. It is not available without a functioning computer system and LAN access.

Reviewing the document indicates that its focus is extremely limited. It would have been completely inadequate in giving direction on September 11. For example, use of telephone is referred to frequently. That would have been impossible. Calling 911 for emergency patient transport would have been fruitless. There has been no official indication of how many patients suffered for lack of service, loss of life-sustaining equipment, no meal delivery, etc. But certainly, none of these contingencies are addressed in the plan. In interviews with senior management, it was made clear that the existing crisis management plan had never been fully developed, never communicated clearly to the staff, and never tested. The success of the agency in handling patients and staff as well as they did that fateful day was a product of OEM training and direction. Management realized that immediate overhaul to the crisis plan was necessary.[28]

Another major concern was the threat of anthrax that followed in the aftermath of September 11. It was the catalyst for management to immediately address the problem of an inadequate crisis management plan. Although management has been responsive, much of the impetus has come from OEM, the Federal Emergency Management Agency (FEMA), and the city and state health departments. Whatever the motivation, the VNSNY has begun to develop a strategy of crisis management more aligned with the sound business principles of crisis management. Crisis is inevitable, and being prepared can help minimize the negative outcomes. Three steps can help organizations handle the crisis more effectively. These include fact gathering, scenario development, and communication. By putting systems in place the agency can be prepared to face a crisis more effectively. The first step was to form a committee to oversee crisis management. Subcommittees have been empowered to address different crisis areas. In addition, the Mailman School of Public Health at Columbia University has been commissioned by city, state, and federal agencies to act in a coordinating capacity with the various health care agencies. All external crisis management plans are being developed with guidance and oversight from this group. This should help give broad coverage to the city for any health emergency that may occur.

In order to witness the extensive changes in crisis management within VNSNY, it will be helpful to look at the Bioterrorism Planning Draft Overview that was developed by a subcommittee of the parent crisis management committee. We can clearly see the comprehensive approach that is being taken. Other committees are developing similar plans to address such potential crises as chemical warfare disruption of, information services, communications, and utilizing appropriate personnel.

Information gathering is a logical first step in developing an effective plan. In the event of bioterrorism, VNSNY would be both a primary and secondary responder. What have we learned from prior historical response? There is a growing area of knowledge about biological agents used against people; what bacteria and viral agents are most likely to be developed as weapons. The Centers for Disease Control and Prevention have developed a PowerPoint presentation on bioterrorism, which it provides to any health care facility that is preparing a response.

VNSNY is using this program as a training tool for staff. It discusses in great detail the important issues particular to the most likely biological agents to be used. Identifying and training nurses on how to handle a crisis is an important consideration. Consider which staff is most likely to participate in the crisis plan, and which will have issues that prevent full cooperation. For example, single mothers are most likely to return home to protect their families. They would not be a considered choice for training. Crisis can sometimes bring to the fore people who can be valuable in unexpected situations. In the aftermath of September 11, information specialists were instrumental in recommendations for the future. The VNSNY has a growing number of Israeli nurses who are experienced in crisis nursing, including use of masks and combat gear. A number of them have offered to participate in training sessions. Their willingness is a valuable asset. Risk management specialists from the legal department should be a part of the committee. Are there liabilities that must be considered?

Communications are vital to the success of any crisis plan. One of the first actions taken by VNSNY after September 11, 2001, was to relocate their computer backup system to New Jersey. Office space for administrators was also rented in New Jersey. The expense is substantial, but deemed necessary to ensure continuity for the organization. Each phase of crisis preparedness will also be communicated to all those who need to know. Contingency plans are in place for relocating the VNSNY offices. Regional offices, however, do not have this option at this time. A system of e-mail, cell phone, and/or beeper communications has been tested.

Planning for potential outbreaks includes predetermination of what might be possible treatment of vaccination sites. Who will order supplies needed to rollout first phase response? What will this cost? Who will pay for supplies, personnel, and vaccines? All of these questions can be explored before a potential crisis. This allows for a quick, decisive response to crisis. Once a plan is formulated, it must be tested and refined as much as possible.

The bioterrorism planning draft is still in the early stages. Once fully developed, it will be integrated into the body of the overall crisis management plan. If fully implemented, it should provide clear, concise direction in the event of a bioattack. Of course, VNSNY is part of the city response system.

No comparison can be made between the pre- and post-September 11 crisis management plan. Even though the new plan is in its infancy, it is more carefully constructed, more comprehensive, and inclusive.

Instead of being written by a single manager, it is a collaborative endeavor by committee and subcommittee. A number of city, state, and federal agencies are resources and partners. The overall plan is being coordinated with the other health care facilities in the metropolitan area. Management is taking a proactive approach to what has become a viable threat to the area served by the agency. This change in crisis management is not necessarily a change in the culture of the organization, but more likely reflective of the dramatic change in the culture of the society it serves. Will this lead to important cultural and organizational changes? The first steps are positive. Management has reached out to all levels for guidance in preparing a cohesive crisis plan. The people who will be most responsible for carrying out the plan are part of the development of that plan. This should provide more universal acceptance and buy-in by staff. It is important to encourage input from all areas of expertise since the crisis potential is outside the box of imaginable scenarios. Progressive, forward thinking is likely to provide new ideas for handling unthinkable crises. VNSNY has not had a history of this type of management. These first steps are encouraging.

CONCLUSION

Above all, crisis management must be viewed as an evolutionary process. In particular, the validity and appropriateness of risk policies need to be reevaluated constantly. In addition, managers must develop, and encourage top management to develop, a crisis management culture and philosophy that permeates the company. They should use crisis to their advantage and reduce the impact of a crisis. So, by being prepared, rehearsing options in advance, developing a crisis plan and identifying communications channels, sales managers can deal successfully with crisis. It is hoped that a crisis management proficiency will help instill the mind-set in managers that a crisis, when handled effectively, is an opportunity to show the marketplace how good they really are.

Chapter 2

Economy

FRAGILITY OF CONFIDENCE

Adaptive change is distressing for the people going through it, and getting an organization to adapt its behaviors to thrive in a changed environment is critical in today's world. The city of New York was hit hard on September 11, 2001, in the midst of battling a possible recession. New York City's economy was affected severely, and a newly elected Mayor Bloomberg was given the task of managing this economic crisis. Mayor Bloomberg states, "The September 11th attack has forced the city to deal with new economic and fiscal conditions. New York City now faces a budget gap for fiscal year 2003 of $4.8 billion."[1]

Major declines in the city's economy linked directly to the attack can mainly be attributed to the loss of 100,000 private sector jobs, the severe decline in New York City tourism, the loss of $800 million in tax payments due to a 60 percent decline in Wall Street profits, and the decline in Manhattan's market value totaling $230 million in lost revenue[2] (see Box 2.1).

Decline in the Real Estate Market

> Nearly 30 million square feet, or almost 30 percent, of the city's Downtown commercial real estate was damaged or destroyed, resulting in the displacement of around 600 firms and an estimated 100,000 people. Firms responded by moving nearly 30 percent of their employees, some permanently, outside the city.[3]

Although the real estate market is being hailed as one of the healthier segments of the city's economy in the current recession, the market was certainly affected in 2001 by job cuts and diminishing confidence

---

BOX 2.1. Economic Effects of September 11 on New York City

General
- The loss of 108,500 private sector jobs
- A severe decline in tourism
- The loss of $800 million in tax payments due to a 60 percent decline in Wall Street profits

Real Estate
- $230 million in lost real estate revenues
- 30 million square feet of commercial real estate deemed inoperable
- 13 million square feet of office space permanently destroyed (World Trade Center)
- Vacancy rates rose as firms offered space for sublease
- 20 to 25 percent reduction in asking rent in the downtown area

Wall Street
- Profits went from $21 billion to $8.5 billion
- Revenues from city taxes declined from $2.6 billion to $1.8 billion

---

in the future business environment. Most of the deterioration has been the result of September 11, although signs of weakness were already apparent in the second quarter of 2001. The loss of 8 percent of primary space in the fourth quarter was a direct result of the destruction of the World Trade Center, as nearly 30 million square feet were permanently inoperable. Of these, approximately 13 million square feet were destroyed permanently. With the loss of that square footage, vacancy rates were expected to decline, however, rates began to rise as many firms anticipating unused space offered it for sublease. The amount of space that suddenly appeared on the market more than offset the amount needed by firms displaced by September 11, as many of them were finding temporary or permanent space outside Manhattan. Many businesses reviewed their real estate needs, canceled expansion plans, and put large, unused blocks of space on the sublet market, causing the first significant decline in asking rents since 1994 (approximately a 20 to 25 percent reduction in the downtown area). "A combination of reduced rents and condo prices, proposed government incentives, and a public spirit desire to participate in the re-birth of downtown is luring new residents to replace the thousands that left." In the fall of 2001, the occupancy rate in Battery Park City dropped to 60 percent.[4]

> For some commercial properties, especially downtown office buildings and hotels citywide, the attack has led to large drops in revenues, which together with the destruction of so much space has cut billable assessments by an estimated $2.3 billion or $230 million in tax levy or payments in lieu of taxes.[5]

Vacancy rates are expected to stabilize as office employment steadies between 2003 and 2006.

Loss of Tax Revenue

A 60 percent decline in Wall Street profits caused a loss of $800 million in potential tax payments. Wall Street's profits went from $21 billion to $8.5 billion, causing the revenues from city taxes to decline from $2.6 billion to $1.8 billion (see Figure 2.1). One week after the attack the Dow fell sharply to its lowest level in three years, the biggest-ever weekly decline. "At the pace of this decline, we were between five and six weeks before the Dow was worth zero," says Pru-

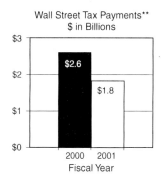

*Estimate
**Includes general corporation, unincorporated business, bank, and personal income tax payments.

FIGURE 2.1. Change in Wall Street Profits from 2000 to 2001

dential market strategist Bob Stovall.[6] In 2003, personal income tax receipts suffered the combined effects of a sharp drop-off in the financial industry real estate (FIRE) sector bonus payout, large employment declines, and a sharp decline in the capital gains realizations in tax year 2001. Personal income tax revenue is forecasted at $4.4 million for 2002, resulting in a collections decline of 17.2 percent from the prior year.

The Decline of New York City's Tourism Industry

The attacks on the World Trade Center have many travel industry experts regrouping and reacting to bring tourists back into New York City. Travel-related businesses were affected across the board. These businesses include air travel, convention centers, restaurants, and hotel sectors. New York City's decline in tourism will not dissolve the city's economy, but it will have a big impact on it.

The travel sector most affected by the attacks is the airline industry (see Box 2.2). Business travel experienced a large decline in fall 2002 when the economy was beginning to slow down. In order to offset the downturn in business travel sales, the airline industry started to hike fares. This did not make up for the lost revenue. The business fares of major carriers increased 70 percent since 1999. Business travel generates the most revenue for the airline industry. Although corporate flyers account for about 43 percent of passenger volume, they generate 65 to 70 percent of revenues and profits. Many companies are chartering flights or buying corporate jets in order to make executives feel comfortable with traveling again. Other companies are replacing face-to-face meetings with digital meetings (Web or conference calls) and finding that they are saving a lot of money in the long run. This is

---

BOX 2.2. New York City Tourism Industries Affected by September 11

- Airlines
- Conference centers
- Restaurants
- Hotels

changing the way that business is done both on Wall Street and world-wide.[7]

New York City's airports were never the most welcoming for business travelers even before the attacks on September 11. Business travelers must now endure even longer delays. More at stake is New York City's reputation as a first-rate location to do business—a reputation that was acquired in the booming economy of the 1990s. It is now more difficult for business travelers to commute into downtown Manhattan.

The convention center sector had also seen a sharp decline in the months following the attacks on the World Trade Center. Convention center attendance depends heavily on air travel and tourism. September and October are the most profitable months for convention center bookings in America's big cities. Attendance is down but is expected to steadily increase throughout the year. After weeks of disruptions following the attack on the World Trade Center, the city's convention center industry is steadily increasing. Convention organizers stated that many meetings and conventions booked prior to September 11 were not canceled, only postponed.

The restaurant industry is slowly rebounding from the attacks on the World Trade Center and the Pentagon. Recent figures are showing that sales nationwide had started increasing.

> Overall sales at eating and drinking places increased 1.4 percent between September and October on a seasonally-adjusted basis after a revised 2.5 percent decline in September, according to preliminary U.S. Census Bureau data. In dollar terms, the sales shortfall is approximately $1 billion.[8]

The restaurant industry's revenue in New York City has also improved since September 11. Some restaurants, depending on where they are located, were affected more so than others. Chinatown is in close proximity to the World Trade Center. After the attacks, streets in Chinatown were closed to pedestrians and vehicles. The restaurants in Chinatown saw "their business drop by 30 to 70 percent."[9] Most restaurant workers in this area were still working on a reduced work schedule months after the attacks.

The hotel sector was also affected by the attacks on the World Trade Center (Figure 2.2).

> The market ended 2001 at 73 percent occupancy and $192 average daily rate—far short of the remarkable numbers achieved in 2000, when occupancies hovered above 80 percent and rates were over $220. This reflects the impact of the World Trade Center attack, as well as the market's inability to sustain levels pre-September 11.[10]

The hotel sector in New York has seen improvements. The Marriott Financial Center has reopened, and Embassy Suites, Ritz-Carlton Battery Park, W Times Square, and Westin Times Square have already opened. New York is slowly starting to rebuild its hotel industry back to where it was up until September 11.

The Loss of Private Sector Jobs

The attack on the World Trade Center in New York City has had a large impact on the loss of jobs in the private sector (Box 2.3). Even before September 11, the economy was faced with a lengthy down-

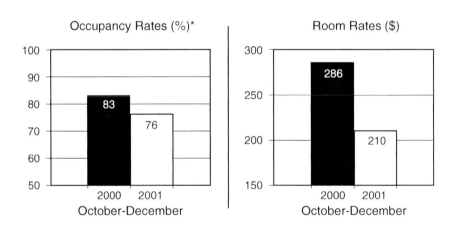

*Occupancy is slowly showing signs of improvement.

FIGURE 2.2. Comparison of Average New York City Hotel Room Rates in 2000 and 2001

BOX 2.3. The Loss of Private Sector Jobs in New York City After September 11

- In an analysis of the mayor's budget 2003, the IBO (Independent Budget Office) "does not expect the city to reach its pre-recession employment peak of—3.8 million jobs—until late 2006."
- Companies are choosing to move to other locations.
- Example of loss of private sector jobs: 7,685 workers were laid off in Chinatown in the first three months following the attack on the World Trade Center. This represents 23 percent of the neighborhood's work force of 33,658.

---

turn. This downturn had forced many companies to lay off employees. Following the terrorist attacks, the possibility of a nationwide recession became a definite reality. With consumers in fear of loss of work, many industries, including retail, tourism, and manufacturing, were affected. The New York City Budget Report shows that the city's employment will not reach full capacity until late in the year 2006 (Figure 2.3).

> After anemic growth of less than 1 percent through most of 2003, payroll employment will grow by 1.4 to 1.5 percent through 2004 (adding 54,000 jobs in 2003 and another 53,000 in 2004), and then settle down to a growth rate of 0.8 percent (about 31,000 jobs per year). IBO does not expect the city to reach its pre-recession employment peak—3.8 million jobs—until late 2006.[11]

The biggest impact of the attacks on job loss has been seen in cities that are heavily dependent on tourism and travel. A recent study conducted by the Milken Institute states that a majority of the economic downfall of the attacks would be focused primarily on tourism sectors. These sectors would include all hotel, restaurant, recreation, and airline industries. "In overall numbers, New York will suffer the most job losses in 2002—nearly 150,000 fewer than it was expected to have in 2002 prior to the events of September 11."[12] (In all, 100,000 jobs were lost in 2002 and 90,000 were lost in 2003.) Tourism gener-

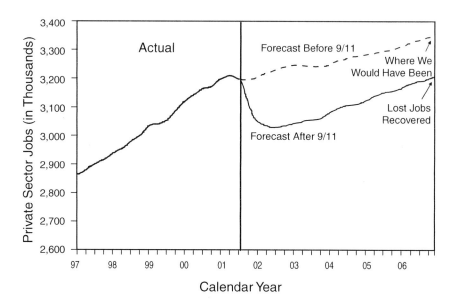

FIGURE 2.3. New York City Will Recover the Lost Jobs by the End of 2006 (*Source:* Actual Data from Bureau of Labor Statistics Non-Agricultural Employment Survey.)

ates many low-skill jobs for New York City. It provides much needed employment opportunities for the poorer segments of the population. Tourism benefits the local economy by bringing in money from outside the city. This generates an additional influx of economic activity.

Another factor affecting job loss is that many companies are choosing to move to another location outside of the city. Although an economic rebound may reverse the downsizing of Wall Street firms, other issues still remain.

> Quality-of-life issues appear to be the impetus from Lower Manhattan, companies are seeking to escape from the still smoldering ruins of the World Trade Center, the awful air pollution, the disabled transportation system and the aging inventory of the office product. It'll be years until those vexing problems are fixed.[13]

Employees that choose not to relocate are faced with losing their jobs.

Chinatown was hit especially hard after the attacks. Many businesses are not able to apply for Small Business Administration loans because they are basically cash based. Due to this, many garment and restaurant workers were laid off.

> According to the report, "Chinatown After September 11th: An Economic Impact Study," 7,685 workers were laid off in Chinatown in the three months after the terrorist attacks on the nearby trade center. The number represents 23 percent of the neighborhood's work force of 33,658.[14]

Although the loss of jobs in New York City has increased in the past several months, the economy is showing signs of improving. The economy is currently moving at a slow pace, but fourth-quarter gross domestic product surprised many experts by showing a small but positive growth. Inflation remains well under control. The housing market is continuing to boom due to low mortgage interest rates. Slowly but surely, New York City's economic situation is improving.[15]

Crisis Management

Could a crisis management team have been able to predict the events following September 11? The answer in most minds is probably no. New York City as well as the rest of the world was not prepared to deal with the impact following the destruction of the Twin Towers. A *crisis* is defined as a major, unpredictable event that has potentially negative results. The results, which have been felt, place a negative impact on the total condition of New York's economy as well as the minds of the people at hand. Mayor Bloomberg had the tough task of having to organize a crisis management team after the crisis had begun. Under normal conditions a team could have prepared the city for a devastating event. Ordinarily, facts could have been gathered to evaluate the situation (see Box 2.4). This is the first step in the process and allows for all relevant information to be released. In this case all information pertaining to potential terrorist attacks would serve a purpose to the team. Some of the other information, which the team may evaluate, includes the current state of the economy, programs to defend the city from potential attacks, and perhaps the internal structure of the city (e.g., the mayor and the police

---

BOX 2.4. The Three Steps in the Crisis Management Process

1: Fact gathering
2: Scenario development
3: Communicating the message

---

commissioner). The internal structure may seem like a simple organizational chart but plays a key role during the time of crisis management. A clear role of decision making must be present during the time of crisis. One must have the authority to make the appropriate decision in a quick and timely manner.

The second step in the crisis management process deals with scenario development. Any individual assigned to handle scenario development could not possibly have considered the devastating events viewed from September 11. It is a difficult task to develop the worst possible scenario. One must make sure to evaluate the worst possible outcome he or she may view potentially for the city. In this case the scenario includes almost 3,000 lives lost and a city that is on edge waiting for the next possible attack. A strong leader is needed during this time to calm the minds of the city and lead them into a stage of recovery. Some of the other potentially negative effects of September 11 include a severe increase in city unemployment, lost tax revenue, and a severe blow to the world's economy. To prepare a back-up plan for one of these circumstances is very difficult, but to plan one for all of these events during the same time frame is nearly impossible. A best-case scenario should also be in the works to allow for quick recovery. When all potential outcomes are evaluated, those who are in charge could take the right steps to make the right decision. This may seem feasible, but it takes months of preparation to evaluate the possible outcomes from the present crisis.[16]

The final stage deals with communicating the message and the decision that the crisis management team has chosen. This is where authority in decision making plays a key role. There cannot be any miscommunications within the organization in order to ensure a proper decision. Mayor Bloomberg has complete faith that these key divisions

(Fire and Police) in his organization (New York City) will come to the best decision in the face of a crisis.

Reengineering

Reengineering serves a major role in rebuilding the most famous city in the world (see Box 2.5). For this process to occur, a radical new design must be formed for the company, or in this case, the city. The emphasis in the process focuses on change with the concept of doing more with less. "In these tough financial times we must learn to do more with less."[17] The mayor has realized what the city needs to do and has responded with the urgency theory as a means to achieve the goal. Some of the advantages viewed with the process include greater productivity and performance within less time, better time management, one-on-one response to urgent demands and decisions required, and the improved ability to develop innovations and ideas. The idea of improved innovations will allow for new programs to be implemented in order to boost the city out of its financial crisis. The significant loss in the city's economy calls for many stimulants to make up for potential lost revenue as well as employment. Mayor Bloomberg has already evaluated the case and offered a $750 million

---

BOX 2.5. Reengineering in New York City After September 11

Goals
- Radical redesign of an organization's operations and management to achieve strategic breakthrough
- Urgency Theory: "Doing more with less"

Efforts to Implement Goals
- Police: Restructuring police force through recruitment and civilization ($43 million)
- Corrections: Closure of Brooklyn Correctional Facility ($4.6 million)
- Sanitation: Temporary termination of metal, glass, and plastic recycling programs ($56.6 million)
- Health: Elimination of research grants ($3 million)
- Libraries: Reduction of library system programs ($39.3 million)

---

investment into housing and development. Under the plan, multifam-
ily housing will be built with a great emphasis being placed on building in the outer boroughs. Commercial and economic development
will also occur under the plan. This is key during a time of rebuilding.
The city knows how important it is to attract corporate investment
into the city and to keep those who exist already. This type of package
lets corporations view the city's long-term outlook. These projected
results will hopefully gain their support. This is one example of the
innovations that are possible under the reengineering idea. Other
ideas being evaluated include new tax proposals as well as tax breaks
for those who remain in the city and conduct their business operations.[18]

Today's post-September 11 business environment calls for "doing
more with less." The mayor sees this as a good choice but will like to
achieve his goal under certain requirements. He views defense as a
very important part in the city's rebuilding process. Following the
events of September 11, who can disagree? In order to accomplish
more, he implemented a plan that brings civilians to the police desk
while desk cops can be out and patrolling. This is a new way to get
more production without having to increase payroll or staff. As far as
the fire department goes, he eliminated overtime staffs and created
seventy-three new jobs and battalion aides in order to help ease the
budget situation within the department. In both cases we are viewing
an increased productivity output by important groups. Some of the
other services, which will face a new design, include the sanitation
department and the health and library services currently available in
the city. Some recycling programs will be dropped to cut the cost of
the production of recycled paper. The health department will cut its
research grants by $3 million in order to operate under a tight budget.
The library system will reorganize under a smaller budget, which will
include the loss of certain services currently available.

Reengineering is a complicated process that needs contributions
from every part of the organization. In the city's case, some departments are contributing by reducing services or by perhaps cutting the
entire program altogether. Every little contribution helps in the new
design that will enable the city to grow. Some of the negative effects
that reengineering had on the city included a decrease in quality production, job burnout, chaotic environment created, too many responsibilities, and the idea of not being able to do more with less. This is

the risk that many organizations are forced to take during a time of turmoil or economic disaster. The results, which followed from taking this chance with a new idea, can create both a positive situation for a company and can perhaps produce a confident and productive new worker.

The Balanced Scorecard

The balanced scorecard is a management system that can motivate breakthrough performance for making requirements. After September 11, it can be used as an effective management tool. The balanced scorecard will tell us where the city stands and what has to be done to improve the situation.

The scorecard translates a business unit's (which in this case is New York City) mission and strategy into a set of measures built around four perspectives. The following are the four areas, which will be discussed and analyzed:

1. Financial: "How do we look to our shareholders?"
2. Customer: "How do we become our customers' most valued supplier?"
3. Internal Processes: "What must we excel at to obtain our objectives?"
4. Innovation and Improvement: "How can we improve and create value?"

Financial: "How Do We Look to Our Shareholders?"

After the September 11 attack, this measurement was very important for Mayor Bloomberg, his team, and the survival of New York City. The measurement shows how people and companies in New York City feel about the current situation and how satisfied they are with its leaders. In this case, the people in the city are the "shareholders" of New York City and the city itself represents a "company."[19]

In a crisis situation, the message about the future outlook is important. How the shareholders think about the company and its future depends on how leaders communicate with them. Mayor Bloomberg showed that he really cares about the city and believes in its future. After the attack, there were many uncertainties. Some of the people in New York City considered moving out of the city out of fear of future terrorist attacks. The companies in downtown New York City were looking to relocate. Wall Street lost a lot of money because of frightened investors, causing the stock market to decline and the economy to weaken. New York City's shareholders need reassurance that the city is heading in the right direction with respect to its economic forecast. If there is confidence in the city's position, shareholders can offer a positive attitude toward the city. Mayor Bloomberg said, "We must work together and find ways to balance our budget as required by law."[20]

Customer: "How Do We Become Our Customers' Most Valued Supplier?"

This measurement explains what the company (New York City) must do internally to meet its customers' expectations. In this case, the customers are people who visit from outside New York City. After the attack, it was important to stay positive and make the city attractive for outside parties. "Although the September 11th attacks dealt a serious blow to our city and its economy, it did not diminish New York City's remarkable strength," said Mayor Bloomberg.[21] The mayor is talking in a positive way, which will attract organizations, tourists, and capital into the city, helping to rebuild New York City and its economy. Tourism has had a significant value to the city's economy and we must do everything to keep it that way. The good news is that the tourism is already up approximately 40 percent from September. Also, there is a plan to build more residential buildings in order to attract more people to move to New York City. The internal communication, commitment, and hard work will help to achieve those goals. It will bring more value to the city, which is needed in these difficult times.

Internal Processes: "What Process—Both Long-Term and Short-Term—Must We Excel at to Achieve Our Financial and Customer Goals?"

The short-term goal for the city is to survive from the attack and balance the budget. After the attack, there was a budget deficit of $4.8 billion. In order to balance the budget, the management must analyze

the current situation, think about the future, and make long-term pre-
dictions.

The city needs to create more jobs, which will eventually bring in
revenue. The city must attract the capital investments, which will help
to grow the economy. Tourism must stay one of the main priorities;
however, in order to attract tourists, the city must be kept safe and
clean.

*Innovation and Improvement: "How We Can Continue
to Improve and Create Value, Particularly in Regard to Employee
Capabilities and Motivation and the Rate of Improvement
of Existing Processes?"*

Many people know New York City as the best city in the world.
This is a great title, which brings value to the city. However, this also
requires constant improvements throughout the city. New York City
has to improve its downtown area (because of September 11), and rebuild the World Trade Center area. The safety of a city is important
and needs constant improvement. The city must be kept clean, and
housing development must be encouraged. New York City needs to
be a friendly place to live and visit.

Budget

New York City will have a financial problem for the next few
years, which means that its revenues do not meet its expenses (Figure
2.4). The budget has to be balanced, however, it has to be done in such
a way that it would not damage the city's infrastructure and its long-
term goals. What happened in New York City should have been predicted for a long time, but unfortunately the city was not prepared for
such an event. After the attack, the economy slowed down, expenses
continued to increase, and tax revenues decreased dramatically, resulting in a budget gap of $4.8 billion in the 2003 fiscal budget, which
began July 1 (Table 2.1). It is very difficult to tell the exact dollar estimate because many uncertainties exist in the current situation and the
future is always hard to predict. The budget gaps for 2004 and 2005
are estimated to be approximately $5 billion and $5.3 billion, respectively, and the 2006 gap will be even higher.[22]

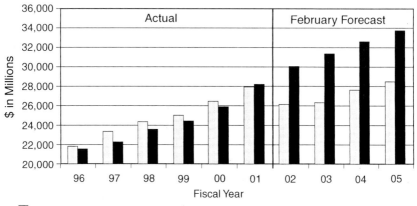

FIGURE 2.4. City Revenues and Expenses Forecast As of February 2002 (*Source:* New York City Budget Report.)

It should not be very difficult to cut $4.8 billion out of the $42 billion city's budget. However, the truth is that it is not easy because the city has control over $14.9 billion only (Figure 2.5). The controllable $14.9 billion is split up by different departments, and some of the areas in the city need money more than others.

The fact is that the budget has to be closed. The city officials decided to close the budget through new taxes and departmental funding reductions. New taxes will help to bring in more revenues. For example, the new cigarette tax will bring in approximately $992 million at the end of 2006. Table 2.2 shows how much each department's budget was reduced in 2003.

As shown, the largest reductions are taking place in the sanitation, correction, and health and welfare departments. Also, a reduction is slated for the mayor's office, which will help to save almost $8 million. Early retirement will be also emphasized and discussed in the next few years. These are the methods that took place in order to close the budget gap of $4.8 billion.

The good news is that the capital commitments for New York City's future remain strong (Figure 2.6). This will help to rebuild the city and its economy. This is a good sign for the future of New York City.

TABLE 2.1. Financial Plan Gap Projection Before Gap Closing Actions

	$ in Millions			
	2002	**2003**	**2004**	**2005**
June 2001 adopted surplus/(gap)	$345	($3,123)	($2,611)	($2,236)
(Increases in gap)/decreases in gap				
Projected expense changes after June 2001 projection	($331)	($564)	($1,576)	($1,952)
State and federal changes from June 2001 projection	(233)	(246)	(266)	(266)
Delay in sale of off-track betting and other nontax revenue changes	(447)	121	226	(37)
Gap prior to revenue loss	($660)	($3,812)	($4,227)	($4,491)
Projected tax revenue decline attributed to 9/11	(792)	(1,303)	(1,176)	(1,255)
Personal income tax cut not enacted	172	349	370	390
Gap to be closed	($1,286)	($4,766)	($5,033)	($5,356)

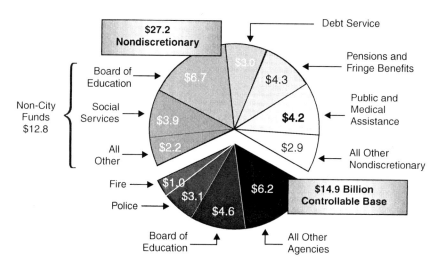

FIGURE 2.5. New York City Budget by Department Allocation (*Source:* New York City Budget Report, 2002.)

TABLE 2.2. New York City Agency Program Allocations (2003)

	Adopted Budget**	(City Funds $ in Thousands)*			Total Reduction (%)
		Expense	Revenue	Total	
Uniformed forces					
Police	$3,033,319	$118,088	$94,088	$212,176	7
Fire	1,025,060	60,029	2,955	62,984	6
Sanitation	981,248	118,856	6,650	125,506	13
Corrections	864,010	102,250	2,000	104,250	12
Health and welfare					
Social Services	3,722,864	53,079	(767)	53,079	1
Administration for Children's Services	743,168	131,857	1,828	133,685	18
Homeless Services	228,434	38,875	—	38,108	17
Public Health	580,064	60,213	1,515	61,728	11
Aging	165,785	26,088	—	26,088	16
Youth and Community Development	86,183	16,548	—	16,548	19
Other mayoral					
Housing Preservation and Development	71,177	10,151	8,530	18,681	26
Finance	191,112	23,187	4,400	27,587	14
Transportation	281,709	11,992	12,292	24,284	9

Parks and Recreation	170,538	19,803	2,150	21,953	13
Citywide Administrative Services	134,677	14,504	13,900	28,404	21
Libraries	262,120	39,318	—	39,318	15
Cultural Affairs	127,518	19,128	—	19,128	15
All Other Agencies	1,251,403	50,926	63,997	114,923	9
Covered organizations					
Board of Education	4,957,146	353,819	7,491	361,310	7
HHC	850,548	11,535	—	11,535	1
CUNY	264,620	12,887	—	12,887	5
Elected officials					
Office of the Mayor	38,771	7,790	—	7,790	20
Borough Presidents	28,665	5,734	—	5,734	20
District Attorneys	231,186	16,226	—	16,226	7
Comptroller	54,599	10,920	—	10,920	20
Public Advocate	2,572	514	—	514	20
City Council	36,630	7,326	—	7,326	20
Grand total	$20,385,126	$1,341,643	$221,029	$1,562,672	8

Source: New York City Budget Report

*Includes January 2002 and November and January 2003 PEGs.
**Adjusted for Mayoralty Reallocations.

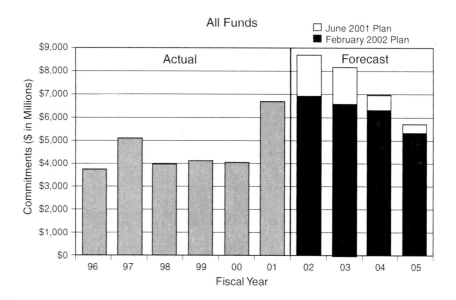

FIGURE 2.6. Capital Commitments for New York City (*Source:* New York City Budget Report.)

Recommendations

Mayor Bloomberg implemented this extensive Budget Gap Closing Program. He has also begun funding to build affordable housing in the boroughs in the interest of sparking the city's economy. However, some areas of importance were ignored such as, the rebuilding of the World Trade Center, city security, and the utilization of Governor's Island to increase city revenue.

To account for the loss of 13 million square feet of office space caused by the destruction of the Twin Towers, a plan to rebuild on that priceless land should begin. While understanding that corporations and the public would feel unsafe in a building that was 110 stories high, an alternative must be evaluated.

Previously occupied by the United States Coast Guard, Governor's Island is 172 acres of land that was bought by New York State from the federal government for a minimal amount of money. President

Bush offered the land, which is said to be worth $500 million, to the state after September 11. Covered with beautiful trees and historic landmarks, with a view of Manhattan's skyline, and equipped with existing docks, Governor's Island could potentially bring in large increments of revenue for the City of New York. The proposal includes converting the land to an upscale "getaway" spot. Beautiful gardens, shops, casinos heavily monitored by the gaming commission, luxurious hotels, and upscale restaurants and clubs will be sure to attract tourists as well as city residents. Currently, people from the tri-state area travel to New Jersey and Connecticut to find casinos. This outflow of dollars could be directed to New York City if a facility of this nature is built. Further, this island would give New Yorkers a means of escape from the hustle and bustle of city life. The island would also attract tourists from around the country who are constantly looking for picturesque views of the city skyline. Developers from as far away as Denmark have already expressed interest in building upon this valuable land.

Last, New York City's current level of security deters commuters as well as tourists from traveling into Manhattan (Box 2.6). Without increasing city expenses, the mayor must find a way to reassure people that New York City is taking every precaution to ensure its safety. Through the use of the National Guard, some of New York's bridges and tunnels have been protected from potential terrorists. However, it is still necessary to take security to a more pronounced level citywide. The National Guard should have a greater presence throughout the city. The National Guard should check all suspicious vehicles passing through tunnels or over bridges twenty-four hours a day. They should

---

BOX 2.6. New York City Security Needs

1. Increase level of security throughout New York City

2. National Guard should have greater presence:

   - Stationed at all bridges and tunnels twenty-four hours a day, seven days a week
   - Checking IDs at entrances of all office buildings
   - Checking every car or truck at the entrance of all parking facilities.

be present at every building's entrance checking IDs of all those who attempt to enter it. They should be at every parking facility, checking every car and truck wanting to park. By increasing security, and publicizing how New York is protected, tourists are expected to feel more confident about visiting. Commuters will also regain the feeling of safety they had prior to September 11, causing more of the workforce to return to companies based in the city.

Annual Forecasts

The city expects to gradually rebuild and recover with the help of the federal and state governments. The recovery of employment and the security industry should grow at a steady rate until 2006. The employment rate increased at the end of 2002 along with the rest of the nation. The employment rate is expected to improve gradually at about 30,000 jobs each year. The city government is hoping that it will level off by 2006. The security industry is also expected to improve. "Following an estimated drop of almost 60 percent in 2001, NYSE member-firm profits are expected to grow at about 10 percent per year in 2002-2006."[23] The profit forecast will increase wage earnings by an average of 5 percent per year until 2006. The commercial real estate market is expected to decline before stabilizing. The market will start to stabilize within the upcoming years. The proposal of the rebuilding efforts of the World Trade Center will gain some of this office space back.

Mayor Bloomberg shows characteristics of a pragmatic leader, one who is a no-nonsense, participatory, quick decision maker with good time-management skills. These abilities along with the combined efforts of the Crisis Management Team will assist in the stabilization of New York City's economy. The mayor must combat the increasing unemployment rate. Some of this has been achieved by bringing tourism back into the city. This will bring in outside revenue and will help small businesses stay afloat during this difficult time. By opening up Governor's Island as a tourist attraction, New York City will become more attractive to tourists wishing to visit. The mayor will assist in the plans of rebuilding of the World Trade Center. The proposal suggests that the city build four buildings, sixty stories high each. This will open up more business space in the downtown area. New York City needs once again to regain the reputation of a good place to do business. Travelers and commuters must feel safe once again to travel into the city. Having the National Guard visible throughout the city will help in the overall safety of travelers and commuters alike. Mayor Bloomberg and the city of New York have an enormous task ahead of them, a task that seemed impossible to overcome only a few months ago. But, the city is already showing signs of improvement as more and more employees are returning to the city to work and more travelers are visiting, Mayor Bloomberg expects New York City to be back on track by year ending 2006 and with the previous proposals in hand, this can be accomplished.

Chapter 3

Airlines

CONSUMER BEHAVIOR PRE–SEPTEMBER 11, 2001

Prior to the terrorist attacks of September 11, 2001, the commercial airline industry was in what could politely be called turmoil or more accurately, a "state of chaos." The industry was marked by a growing list of consumer complaints and disenchantment. The flying public was forced to contend with numerous issues, such as ever-increasing delays, a sharp spike in ticket costs, the phenomena of "air rage" in which violent/rowdy passengers disrupt flights, frequent management squabbles with organized labor unions, lost passenger luggage, rude airport and flight crew service, and fewer choices of airlines. In all, the 582.3 million passengers who annually flew on domestic carriers were encountering an increasingly stressful and costly experience.

A dominant factor in customer dissatisfaction with the industry in general was the lack of choices in the consumer air travel market. As a result of business conditions, consumers were faced with fewer choices among airlines and flight schedules. "The major airlines, including US Airways and United, announced plans to merge into monopolistic mega-carriers (the result being fewer choices) and in many cases, reduce service (the result being less-convenient schedules)."[1] Recent years have seen the collapse of leading airlines such as Pan American (bankruptcy and Chapter 7 liquidation), Eastern (bankruptcy in 1991), and Trans World (bankruptcy and assets were purchased by American Airlines in 2001).[2]

In 1999, the number of consumer complaints to the Transportation Department concerning the ten major U.S. carriers more than doubled, ballooning to 13,709 from 5,808 in 1998. This increase in customer complaints occurred as the number of passengers on those carriers increased by about 16 million between 1998 and 1999 to 553.8 million, a growth of about 3 percent, according to Transportation Department figures. Customer complaints could include such things as scheduling, overbooking, fares, baggage, and service. The ten airlines themselves reported more than 2.5 million consumer complaints about lost or damaged luggage.

A major focus of traveler disdain in 1999 was America West Airlines, which had the highest rate of passenger complaints received at the Transportation Department, nearly four for every 100,000 passengers served. The average for all ten major airlines was roughly 2.5 complaints for every 100,000 passengers. Most of the America West complaints related to the cancellation and delay of flights, and if air travelers took attendance, the airline would have been punished for chronic lateness. America West, based in Phoenix, Arizona, had the poorest on-time arrival record of any major airline in 1999, with almost a third of its flights pulling up to terminal gates in excess of fifteen minutes behind schedule.[3]

Concerns of Customers and Providers

Trans World Airlines (TWA) stood at the "head of the class," with close to 81 percent of its flights delivering passengers to their destinations on time, according to the Air Travel Consumer Report 2001 issued by the Inspector General of the U.S. Department of Transportation.[4] The Transportation Department report does not specify the reasons for flight delays, which might be caused by factors such as severe weather, air traffic control decisions, passenger problems, or equipment failures. The report showed that less than 70 percent of America West's flights arrived on time in 1999. The airline also had the most arrival delays in 1998.

Passenger rights became a hot topic among federal legislators on Capitol Hill in 1999. Representative Bud Schuster (R-PA) proposed a passenger bill of rights to meet many of the concerns of the flying public. Representative Schuster's bill mandated that the airlines:

- pay passengers kept waiting on the runway for more than two hours;
- give refunds for flights canceled for economic reasons;
- explain the reasons for delays, diversions, or cancellations; and

- reveal the number of flights available for frequent-flyer redemption.

On the other side of Congress, Senators John McCain (R-AZ), Ron Wyden (D-OR), and Richard Bryan (D-NV) introduced their own Airline Passenger Fairness Act. This act requires airlines to:

- enable passengers to find out if a flight is oversold;
- set up a twenty-four-hour deadline to deliver baggage;
- provide information on all possible fares; and
- grant refunds if ticket-holder cancels within forty-eight hours.

Ultimately, Congress, due largely to intense pressure applied by the industry's lobbying association and the airlines' decision to create a series of self-regulatory policies, adopted none of these measures.[5]

To reduce the congressional impulse toward regulation, the Air Transport Association (ATA), an association of the fourteen largest commercial carriers, created the Customer First program. The key parts of the plan were intended to improve the availability of airfare and flight delay information to airline passengers, call for a government review of liability limits for lost luggage, address emergency situations involving long delays, and improve airline responsiveness to complaints.

Under the plan, each carrier developed individual customer service plans, which included the following provisions:

- *Inform passengers of the lowest fare available.* Each ATA airline would quote the lowest available fare for which the customer is eligible on the airline's telephone reservation system for the flight and class of service requested.
- *Delay notification.* Airlines would notify customers of known delays, cancellations, and diversions. Each airline would establish and implement policies and procedures for notifying customers at the airport and on board affected aircraft of information regarding delays, diversions, and cancellations in a timely manner.
- *Complaints.* Each airline would assign a customer service representative, responsible for handling passenger complaints and ensuring that all written complaints are responded to within sixty days.

- *Increase baggage liability limits.* ATA airlines would petition the Department of Transportation within thirty days for an increase in the current baggage liability limit of $1,250 per bag.
- *Meet customers' essential needs.* During long on-aircraft delays, ATA airlines would make every reasonable effort to provide food, water, restroom facilities, and access to medical treatment for onboard passengers who are on the ground for an extended period without access to the terminal.
- *Disclose airline policies to consumers.* Each airline would make available the following to their customers: cancellation policies resulting from failure to use each flight coupon; rules, restrictions, and an annual report on frequent flyer programs; and upon request, information regarding airline seat size and pitch.

In January 2000, the Transportation Department's Office of the Inspector General began accepting complaints from consumers concerned about airline overbooking and ticket prices. Concerning reports of mishandled bags, United Airlines had the worst record, with 543,491 complaints. Southwest Airlines had the lowest rate of complaints overall in 1999, with only 0.4 for every 100,000 air travelers. This airline also had the lowest percentage of reports concerning bags that were damaged, lost, or delayed. In 1998, Southwest Airlines had been the on-time arrival winner but slipped to number 2 in 1999 with an 80 percent on-time record. Almost in a dead heat with Southwest, Northwest came in third for on-time arrivals, a major improvement for the airline that had ranked number 9 in 1998. The ten air carriers were Alaska Airlines, America West Airlines, American Airlines, Continental Airlines, Delta Airlines, Northwest Airlines, Southwest Airlines, Trans World Airlines, United Airlines, and US Airways.

Long delays on departing flights were one of the most important issues of concern to air travelers. In June 2000, United Airlines alone reported a total of nearly 6,000 flight cancellations, which stranded passengers for an indefinite period of time. That same month, according to the Department of Transportation, consumers registered nearly 2,400 complaints regarding flight delays.[6]

To help alleviate delays and improve service, Congress appropriated $40 billion in September 2000 dedicated to improvements at airports and the air traffic control system in the United States. Part of the funding of the so-called "AIR 21" program was aimed at improving sixteen runway expansion projects underway at the nation's top twenty-five airports.

According to a report released in February 2001 by the U.S. Department of Transportation's Inspector General's Office, airlines were making great progress in addressing such customer concerns as quoting the lowest airfare and responding to complaints promptly, but they provided "untimely, incomplete, or unreliable reports" about flight delays and cancellations.[7]

The report was the culmination of more than a year of work by the Department of Transportation's watchdog branch. More than forty people in the Inspector General's Office participated in the study, observing approximately 550 delayed and 160 canceled flights, reviewing 4,100 baggage claims and placing nearly 2,000 phone calls to reservation centers. The report made twenty-nine recommendations to the airlines, the Department of Transportation, and Congress, including:

- Making the voluntary customer service commitments enforceable by law or regulation. "Three of the 14 airlines have already taken action to incorporate all provisions of the commitment and their plans into their contracts of carriage," the report said.[8]
- Airlines should establish targets for reducing the number of chronically delayed and/or canceled flights.
- Airlines should also provide on their Internet sites the prior month's on-time performance for each scheduled flight.

In response to the Department of Transportation's report, the fourteen largest airlines, through the Air Transport Association, took the public relations initiative to customer service by introducing a plan of commitments to the public. The notable items were:

1. Take steps to ensure that customers are aware of the lowest fare available when purchasing tickets at airport ticket counters and airline ticket offices.
2. Work to ensure that passengers can determine if their flights are on time, delayed, or canceled before they depart for the airport.
3. Commit additional efforts to ensuring that passengers' concerns are heard and addressed, particularly those with special needs and disabilities.
4. Form a task force including representatives of airlines, airports, and the Federal Aviation Administration to review and make

recommendations that will help ensure airport display monitors and other information customers receive are accurate and timely.

5. Establish performance measurement systems to comply with their respective plans.

Implications to Airlines

As the summer travel season drew to a close in September 2001, the airlines and the American public were seemingly obsessed with the idea of making air travel as quick, reliable, and comfortable as possible. As indicated in the surveys cited earlier, most consumers indicated that their leading concerns were delays, expense, customer service, and lost luggage. Although some surveys indicated a modest increase in consumer confidence in the commercial carriers, the ATA's leadership frequently found itself at odds with academic studies of consumer sentiment. In response to the release of The Airline Quality Rating 2001 by the University of Nebraska at Omaha and Wichita State University, the Air Transport Association resoundingly took issue with the report. ATA President and CEO Carol Hallett stated, "It is disingenuous for these universities to ignore the tremendous progress achieved by our airlines over the past two years. . . . This report, as in previous years, is nothing more than bad information that misleads consumers."[9]

After the events of September 11, the concerns of consumers, airlines, and the government changed dramatically.

THE IMMEDIATE IMPACT OF SEPTEMBER 11 ON THE TRAVEL INDUSTRY

On September 20, 2001, Treasury Secretary Paul O'Neill commented that "We don't really know how big a shock it is going to be, or how long it will last."[10]

One of the first markets to be hit was the commercial airline industry, whose planes were unfortunately involved as the weapons of destruction in this attack. As the overall industry scrambled to reassign flights, calm passengers, and convince its employees that the skies were safe, the overall loss amounted to $1.4 billion in the four-week aftermath to right the immediate damage done to current flyers—both business and leisure travelers.

To cope with the damage of September 11, business and leisure travelers began to find alternate ways to cope with the necessity of flying, such as via bus, automobile, or rail. The statistical effects of these trends from September 2000 to September 2001 can be seen in the following chart formed with data provided by the U.S. Department of Transportation's Bureau of Transportation Statistics, which tracks and compares monthly sets of data.

	Domestic (%)	International (%)
Revenue passenger miles	−32	−29
Available seat miles	−19	−15
Passenger load factor	−10	−13
Aircraft revenue departures	−21	−19

In the immediate aftermath of September 11, it is quite evident that consumers were gripped with fear and reacted unfavorably to air transportation as a whole. This reaction prompted an immediate financial crisis within the airline industry as 50,000 job layoffs or furloughs were announced within two weeks of the attacks in addition to another 30,000 workers from Boeing, the world's largest aircraft maker. Although flights were being reduced due to a lack of consumer demand, companies were also reacting to customer concern by reviewing measures to better prepare their flight staff and further safety measures.[11]

One of the first airlines to act with the safety of its passengers and staff in mind was JetBlue, a relative newcomer to the air industry. The New York City-based airline was the first airline to begin steps to replace the cockpit door with a bulletproof version, with added safety features, in all of their aircraft to further protect pilots from threat of an attack and a cockpit seizure. To further safety while the plane is in flight, top House of Representatives members plan to introduce legislation to allow commercial pilots to voluntarily carry firearms into the cockpit with them. Other measures currently being reviewed include allowing stewardesses to carry stun guns and adding more manpower to the federal air marshall program by placing a watchful eye in every flight. While these plans were in the making, much more immediate action was being taken in airports around the country and world-wide.[12]

A quick survey taken by Boeing of its top customers gathered the best choices to improve security that included measures to be taken outside of the aircraft (Boeing/Wirthlin Survey). This practice was implemented immediately as airlines began to take action by increasing baggage screening and providing a more qualified and trained security staff.[13]

These policies were swiftly enacted with the help of the U.S. Department of Transportation under the guidance of Norman Mineta. In a speech to the U.S. Chamber of Commerce summit, Mineta commented that the Aviation and Transportation Security Act of 2001 would continue to make progress with advanced technology and training to place travelers' minds at ease. Immediate reaction included increased X-ray screening and random baggage checks of travelers as they prepared to board planes. With the help of federal funding, Mineta envisions a mix of explosive detection equipment in all of the 429 commercial airports in the country. He also awarded a contract to Lockheed Martin Services for $105 million to train the now federally controlled force of 32,000 airport passenger and baggage screeners.

Chapter 4

Airline Consumers

THE CONSUMER

The typical traveler utilizes airlines for business or leisure travel. Therefore, the effects of September 11 caused these two types of consumers to reevaluate their want to travel and the need for air travel to get them there. In general, consumers reacted favorably to the overall increased security measures, but were unprepared for the delays caused by long lines at security checkpoints and hassle of random baggage checks at the gate. In addition, the Boeing survey taken in November 2001 found that nine out of ten Americans who traveled commercially after September 11 felt safe or very safe due to the increased security at airports, whereas 3 percent said air travel is now too big of a hassle to endure.

One of the most formidable sources for consumer behavior in regard to leisure and business travel is the *National Travel Monitor* reported by Yesawich, Pepperdine and Brown/Russell YPB&R. This marketing services firm regularly monitors consumer attitudes toward travel in the form of a survey. This firm conducted three rounds of surveys in the months of October 2001, November 2001, and January 2002, as well as an April 2002 report that revealed the aftershocks of September 11 seem to be receding in the travel industry. In addition, a working group of travel agents and airlines unveiled the Flight Plan for America as a campaign through public education to reassure travelers of the efforts made to improve airline security and to encourage travel.[1]

According to a survey conducted by Flight Plan for America, of more than 1,000 travel agents to assess the current business environment for the first half of 2002, the two primary reasons to continue traveling are for business and leisure activities. Other reasons included the need for vacation coupled with the availability of large travel discounts, and a small percent (1.5 percent) cited the need to "make a statement" against terrorism. However, fear still lingers in leisure travelers who prefer to stay close to home rather than attempt travel despite better security measures. In fact, the Travel Industry Association of America estimates that trips by personal car in 2004 will increase by 3 percent, whereas travel by plane will decrease almost 4 percent. This figure brings to light the issue of how Americans will travel as opposed to whether they will travel at all. The Flight Plan for America group encourages travelers to continue to travel by whatever means possible and cites a change in travel habits and preference as noted in the following lists:

Types of Travel That Have Increased

Car travel   plus 51%
Getaways closer to home   plus 50%
Domestic trips   plus 32%
Rail travel   plus 21%
Motorcoach tours   plus 8%
Family travel   plus 8%

Top Five Expected Changes in Travel Preference

1. Domestic trips
2. Cruise vacations
3. Visiting family and friends
4. Family vacations
5. Escorted tours

These figures are complemented by the survey conducted by YPB&R in the *National Travel Monitor* that reveals 36 percent of leisure travelers took more trips in 2003, whereas only 25 percent of travelers will take fewer or no trips.[2] Nearly four in ten business travelers cite company restrictions as the reason they will be traveling less. With the effects of the economy in the wake of September 11, companies are finding alternate ways to conduct business without the need for costly air travel and accommodations. In addition, the survey found that the typical "road warrior" with a family has elected to utilize technology for videoconferencing or Webcasting in an effort to stay closer to home and avoid the skies.[3]

With increased technological developments in this area and the rising cost of flying, companies are resorting to this technique to cut cost and comply with the wishes of their employees. In comparison to the business type, *Condé Nast Traveler* magazine surveyed its readers via e-mail and found that 87 percent were willing to fly domestically and 83 percent would travel internationally. This can be coupled with the results from YPB&R that found the top vacation destinations to be Florida (40 percent) and California (38 percent) domestically, whereas Europe, Australia, and the Caribbean were the top international destinations at 71 percent, 25 percent, and 18 percent, respectively.[4]

GOVERNMENT ASSISTANCE AND BUSINESS REFORMS

To aid in the recovery of the travel industry, many are turning to the government for economic assistance. The American Society of Travel Agents received assistance in the form of low-interest or no-interest loans totaling close to $4 billion dollars to stabilize the travel and tourism industry and give back to financially strapped businesses. The nine-month program would establish a $100 million dollar grant program to provide funds for state travel and tourism offices to promote travel. However, members of Congress insist that the program is intended to be a "shot in the arm" to the industry and not an entitlement program.

Those in the travel and tourism industry feel encouraged to push for more funding as assistance, believing that agents will be heavily utilized in the wake of September 11. According to Melinda Bush in an article for *Hotel and Motel Management Magazine,* travelers will need more assurance, more advice, and more service when planning their travel needs.[5] However, according to the *2002 American Express Leisure Travel Index,* more consumers are looking online but booking with known agents.[6] This is in sharp contrast with a benchmark survey issued by GetThere.com which reports a 45 percent increase in online bookings for business travelers. GetThere.com says companies are saving an average of 46 percent by booking online, whereas major corporations report an average savings of 14 percent.[7]

In an effort to gain a part of this online blitz, major airlines such as Northwest, American, and others joined to promote competitive bidding for this share of the consumer market and formed Orbitz. However, many companies also reported a decrease in their travel budgets. No matter whether they are booking online or through a travel agent, customers are now looking to get more out of the total travel experience, from the planning to the trip experience. Flight Plan for America, by surveying their travel agents, found an anticipated increase in domestic trips closer to home, safe and complete package cruise vacations with an overall increase in more family vacations and escorted tours. Regardless, *Travel Agent Magazine* contributor Kathleen Cassidy recommends a new focus on overall consumer satisfaction and recommends adding more value by providing quality experiences. Although she recognizes that some companies may be pressured by budget cuts, with the increase in private online bookings and discount travel, research shows that the U.S. consumer is unwilling to give up travel luxury products.

After September 11, the overall effects of that one horrible day on the airline industry can be assessed. While some in the air travel industry have not survived, such as U.S Airways, others were able to weather the storm, including Virgin Atlantic who was able to return to full time the 600 employees put on part-time service, as opposed to being laid off. Carriers and service providers, including travel agents and tourism spots, will continue to push for further federal funding to promote travel, whereas consumer and industry groups will assess the security conditions under which we travel.[8]

In accordance with the U.S. Department of Transportation's suggestions, travel overall will become safer as more people return to traveling. In essence, the wave of fear that swept the United States has subsided and the travel industry is making a recovery while implementing strategies to improve customer service to retain current customers and attract a new customer base of online shoppers and discount fare searchers.

Looking Toward the Future: Strategies Used by the Airlines

The main reason why the airline recovery is happening so slowly is the discount fares being offered in the wake of September 11. According to American Airlines beginning in 2001 they were seeing heavier passenger loads. According to Al Becker, spokesman at American Airlines, "The problem the industry has is there's a lot of discount fares, and so we are not making money."[9]

In the months following September 11, 2001, the airline industry thought the main way to entice their customers back was to lower fares. As of March 2002, this strategy seemed to be working. The passenger load on their planes had steadily increased. The problem is that the airlines are recovering very slowly because of these discount fares, and that begs the question: Can they afford to keep offering services at these prices?

An article in *The New York Times* reported that, traditionally, business travelers accounted for 40 percent of the airline revenue. Business travelers have been using other means of transportation "with the economic downturn, and with the increased perception of security delays at airports after Sept. 11, many business travelers have chosen not to travel or to use alternative transportation."[10]

The airline industry thinks that by overhauling its complex airfare system it can come up with fares that will be more fairly distributed between the leisure flier and the business flier. Industry executives are hoping that they can raise fares and not decrease the current passenger load. Consumer advocate Joe Brancatelli does not think passengers will find value in a system such as this. "At a certain point, if you didn't price your product not only fairly but what the customer perceives as fair, you will fail," said Mr. Brancatelli, an advocate of lower fares for business travelers. "You can't sustain losses like this forever. And you can't sustain a system like this forever. The market has said no."[11]

The problem with this approach is that the airlines are looking at one specific feature of the reasons why or why not a business traveler would choose to use an airplane as a means of transportation. The driving forces that will make the customer purchase a service or product is *value*. Is the monetary value of the services the only thing that these consumers value when it comes to choosing whether to fly? Declining corporate budgets are playing a role in the funding given to employees for business trips. "A survey of 184 companies and large organizations, released by the Business Travel Coalition in April, showed that 74 percent of participants said their travel budget cuts were permanent."[12]

A research report in *The New Times* states that two of the biggest airline carriers, Delta and Continental, have decided to raise their fares for the leisure traveler by $20 per roundtrip ticket.

According to Tom Parsons, chief executive of Bestfares.com: "With the lack of high-paying business travelers, the burden to make an airline profitable now falls on the group that is flying—the discretionary leisure travelers."[13]

Airlines are not raising fares for the business class, but they are raising rates for the leisure traveler to try to increase their profit margin. They are treating these two customers differently and they feel that the needs of the leisure flier are different from those of business travelers. The business traveler is probably more concerned about being on time. The leisure traveler is more worried about having a good vacation.

A big concern that air travelers still have the safety of flying. The federal government has taken numerous measures to make air travel safer. Government provisions have worked toward safer conditions, but now, officials are talking about adding additional measures. The more measures that are added, the longer it will take to search each person thus delaying flights and causing people to wait longer at airports. The top officials of 39 airports, which handle most of the nation's air travelers, warned the secretary of transportation that air travel would be seriously disrupted in January 2002 unless Congress delayed the December 31, 2002, deadline for screening all checked bags, a major defense against terrorism. As of June 3, 2002, the Bush Administration will be holding to the current deadline for the security measures to be installed. The Bush Administration turned aside a call by airport and airline officials to reconsider a December 31 deadline for mandatory screening of all checked baggage.

The airlines and the airport management were concerned about this deadline for several reasons. It cut down on the number of flights per day an airline can complete and may also reduce profits. Another big problem is how this would affect the customer. One of the things discussed was situational influence. Of course this is not a shopping environment but the more uncomfortable people are at airports, the more likely they will be to choose an alternative mode of transportation in the future. Under the concept of Total Quality Management, "speed" is listed as a major dimension. A slowdown in the boarding process will cause longer lines at the airport. This will also lead to people having to be at the airports earlier in order to be able to board the plane on time. At Hartsfield-Jackson Atlanta International Airport, a spokeswoman predicted "'mass congestion and confusion that will make passengers drive."

Since the airlines do not have any real control over actions taken by the federal government, other approaches may be taken to make its customers have a more pleasant experience at the terminals. Moods are very important. Two dimensions make up a mood—pleasure and arousal—and if the experience is negative the person will remember that and have a negative opinion of that service. It is crucial that passengers have a pleasant experience.[14]

Another problem with the new screening system is that the government is having trouble getting the big machines wired in time and able to scan luggage quickly. As people are waiting in line perhaps the airline can offer complimentary nonalcoholic beverages. In cold-weather climates, offering hot beverages to warm the passengers might be a nice touch. Or the airlines could possibly chip in and get heated overhangs for passengers who are stuck outside the airport doors. For those hot summer days one could hand out water bottles and fans for the passengers to cool themselves. An airliner logo could be printed on the bottle so it serves as advertising.

The airport is not the only place that the airline industry is vulnerable. With today's modern technology airliners are also vulnerable while they are in the air. There have been reports of the U.S. military finding handheld Russian anti-aircraft missiles in Afghanistan. The FBI warns that Americans should be cautious because they think that Al-Qaeda may continue to target commercial airliners.

> Some thirty Russian-made missiles were discovered in the area of Khost-Gardez. The find follows a warning from the FBI that terrorists may try to use such missiles against U.S. targets, especially commercial planes. The FBI alerted law enforcement agencies of the possibility after investigators concluded Al Qaeda operatives might have tried to shoot down a U.S. military plane in Saudi Arabia. . . .[15]

With developments such as this it is interesting that people still continue to fly. Airplanes fill a need: when a customer desires to get to a destination quickly, the airliner is the quickest form of transportation.

Although it does seem that the airlines, through cheap fares, have found a way to get people back up and flying, it seems that some customers are deciding to use railways instead of planes. "The clear recent success of Amtrak's Northeast corridor rail system, and especially of the high-speed Acela trains that share it, is usually treated as an incidental consequence of the catastrophe of September 11."[16]

One question that could be asked is: Why is the consumer behaving in this manner? Is it September 11 that is causing the move to the railroads or is it the efficiency of high-speed trains that is causing the switch. Mr. Bartels suggested: "It has nothing to do with romance," he said. "It's about business and the vaunted American productivity. In the United States, you can simply no longer justify the economic costs and lost productivity of traveling short distances by air."[17] Delta's new commercials offer some very attractive features to the business traveler for their shuttle services. Their promotion theme is that planes are more efficient than trains (see Box 4.1).

Obviously, Delta is trying to zero in on their customers' need for quick and efficient travel. On average, Delta is claiming that the airplane is about three times faster than traveling on the superfast trains. They also claim that they offer the customer more features with this service than the train does. For example, they are offering four differ-

---

BOX 4.1. Delta Airlines Advertisement

Planes Are Faster Than Trains

Triple base miles and double guarantees

- **Triple Base Miles on Every Flight**
  Get Triple Base Miles every time you fly the Delta Shuttle through August 31, 2002. As an added bonus, these miles will count toward Medallion qualification.

- **20 Minute Check-In and Seat Guarantee**
  From check-in to gate in 20 minutes or less or you get 20,000 bonus miles. And, only Delta Shuttle guarantees you a seat! On Shuttle flights between Boston and New York-La Guardia and between Washington-Reagan and New York-La Guardia through June 30, 2002.

ent ways to check in: curbside, kiosk, wireless, and phone. On the plane they offer more leg room, snacks, coffee, and other amenities. On the ground they are offering comfortable lounges, Bloomberg Stock Quotation Terminals, copy and fax machines, personal computers, complimentary newspapers and magazines, morning coffee and juice bar available free of charge to all Delta Shuttle customers. This is a big dilemma for the airlines.[18]

As mentioned earlier, business travelers account for 40 percent of airline ticket sales. If they lose business travelers, airlines that are already losing money will continue to do so. The airlines must discover why this is a growing trend in the United States. Delta has taken steps to try to lure business back to its planes with its new advertising campaign.

Time will tell whether the services that Delta is offering are good enough to bring satisfaction to those who have made the move from the airplane to the train. Since high-speed trains are a popular way of traveling from city to city in Europe, perhaps this shift in consumer behavior is long overdue in the United States.

One way in which the airlines can get an idea of how their customers might be better accommodated if these security measures are put into place is to survey their frequent fliers. A benchmark survey could be used here because it is more comprehensive than the transactional survey and not done after every flight. A customer advisory board in this case might also be a good idea. Current customers of the airlines and those who switched from using planes to using trains could serve on such a board.[19]

The government is obviously assuming that the flying public is demanding new safety regulations while the airlines are using lower fares to entice customers to fly again. Evidence indicates these are two features that customers are now considering when flying. Is the airport doing a good enough job, checking luggage for suspicious objects and does the price of the ticket give value to the travel? The question of whether satisfaction is an emotion is discussed in Richard Oliver's research book, *Satisfaction.* The author seems to feel that it is a component of consumption.[20] This may be the case in the decision-making process of whether to fly.

Chapter 5

Airline Overview

OVERVIEW OF THE AIRLINE INDUSTRY

The airline industry plays a significant role in the U.S. economy. Before the September 11 tragedy, the U.S. airline industry employed 621,000 people and generated 3 percent of the gross domestic product, which was almost $273 billion (Air Transport Association).[1] The average employee income was nearly $64,000.

The airline industry can be classified into three categories based on the amount of revenue the airlines generate. The first category includes the major airlines that annually generate operating revenues in excess of $1 billion. In 2000, there were twelve major passenger airlines and three all-cargo airlines in the United States. The passenger airlines were as follows: Alaska, America West, American, American Eagle, American Trans Air, Continental, Delta, Northwest, Southwest, Trans World, United, and US Airways. The all-cargo airlines included DHL Airways, FedEx, and United Parcel Service.[2]

The second category includes national carriers that generate operating revenues between $100 million and $1 billion. These airlines serve particular regions of the country. The airlines in this category were, for example, Aloha, Atlas Air, Emery Worldwide, Evergreen, Hawaiian, Midwest Express, and Polar Air Cargo. The third category includes airlines that generate operating revenues from $20 million to $100 million. These are regional carriers with service limited to a single region of the country (Air Transport Association).[3]

Factors Influencing the Airline Industry

The situation in the airline industry has changed significantly since the year 2000; however, the current situation is not only a result of the

September 11, 2001, tragedy. In fact, the airlines have been in trouble since the year 2000.

Several variables have been affecting the airlines for the past two years. It is hard to say which of the reasons has had the most significant impact on the situation in the airline industry. Rather, it can be the combination of all the reasons that affects the industry now.

First, in late 2000, the airlines started to lose the business travelers who are their most lucrative customers. It was the consequence of firms trying to cut cost as the economic downturn started to prevail. In fact, the cost of air travel is one of the expenses the companies can decrease the fastest. Between 1996 and 2001, the prices for business travel increased by 76 percent. For example, Delta round-trip fares from Atlanta to San Francisco jumped from $1,216 to $2,048.[4]

In addition, the difference between business and leisure prices increased. According to Northwest, 15 percent of the traffic comes from unrestricted business customers who make up 40 to 66 percent of the revenue. Moreover, fares for business travelers are now twice as high as those for leisure travelers compared to the beginning of the 1990s when it was only 12.5 times as high. As a result of a strong economy, it was easy to fill the planes with corporate travelers. An escalation in airline bills led the companies to switch to teleconferencing and videoconferencing in order to save money. As a result, the airlines' business travel decreased 30 percent January to December 31, 2001. Therefore, the airlines tried to attract leisure travelers to replace the business lost as a result of business travel decline. However, it became impossible. Consequently, even before the September 11 disaster, the industry was already losing between $2.5 billion and $3.5 billion. In fact, it was the worst performance of the industry since 1992.

Second, the airlines must face high fixed costs for airplanes, salaries, and fuel. In fact, 75 percent of fixed-cost spending goes toward paying for airplane leases, interest payments, and labor. The jet fuel prices have skyrocketed since 1999. In 1999, the jet fuel price was $10 a barrel; by 2000, the price reached $22 a barrel.

Moreover, salaries for pilots are high, which forces the ticket prices up. There is a large difference between the maximum pilot salary at the major airlines and the maximum salary at the low cost airlines. For example, the maximum pilot salary is $290,000 at United compared to $148,000 at Southwest and $81,000 at American Eagle. The average amount of flight hours per month was eighty for the United and American Eagle pilots compared to eighty-five for Southwest. Furthermore, in a statement made by Senator Earnest F. Hollings, Democrat of South Carolina, the airlines were giving their executives $120 million in salaries and bonuses during 2001.

The unions in the airline industry are very powerful; it is very costly for the airlines to have their pilots on strike. In fact, a one-month walkout by pilots can wipe out a year's profits. In 2003 pilots at United Airlines and Delta Air Lines won large wage increases. Therefore, it was assumed that American had to match such pay rates. In July, American offered to increase the salary for pilots by 15 to 22 percent beginning August 31. This proposal was not accepted at that time. Negotiations across the whole airline industry have become very long and adversarial.[5]

In addition, the debt load increased significantly during the second half of the 1990s. In the mid-1990s the airlines experienced one of the most prosperous periods in their history. Between 1995 and 2000 the airlines earned $23 billion. At the same time, they achieved only an 8 percent return on capital. For comparison, the auto industry managed a return on capital of 10 percent. When firms are prosperous, they increase their debt. This is what happened to the airlines. In the late 1990s, the airlines total debt load reached $30 billion, which is almost equal to total equity of the airline industry. As a result, the returns for airlines suffered from the large interest payments on the debt.[6]

As described earlier, the airline industry was already vulnerable before the attacks on September 11. Due to high fixed costs, the airlines can mount losses very quickly when demand drops. This is exactly what happened on and after September 11. All planes were grounded for the first time ever. Commercial jets are very expensive; therefore, the airlines try to keep them in the air as much as possible to earn money. On the morning of September 11, 4,000 to 4,500 planes were in the sky. Hundreds more were waiting for departure. Many planes were forced to land at airports they were not familiar with. All these facts caused a problem the airlines have never encountered before. In fact, the airlines had virtually no revenue for three to four days after the tragedy. As a consequence of the grounding, the industry as a whole lost approximately $200 to $300 million a day.

THE AFTERMATH OF SEPTEMBER 11

Downsizing was the most evident result of the airline industry situation. Layoffs occurred through almost the entire industry. Continental Airlines was the first major airline to announce extensive layoffs. Continental announced 12,000 employees would immediately lose their jobs, which was more than 20 percent of its workforce.[7]

Next to announce sweeping layoffs was United, which was downsizing 20 percent of its workforce or about 20,000 employees. United was followed by American Airlines, which announced job cuts for 20,000 employees, and Northwest, which disclosed 19 percent reduction in its workforce. Delta was expected to lay off more than 10,000 employees. The only airline that did not announce layoffs was Southwest.

Smaller airlines also faced layoffs. Frontier Airline, based in Denver, announced a job cut of 440. Milwaukee-based Midwest Express decided to cut 450 jobs. Drastic reductions in the labor force are summarized in the following list:

Airline	Previous Workforce	Job Cuts Announced
American and TWA	138,500	20,000
United	100,500	20,000
Delta	81,000	13,000
Continental	56,000	12,000
US Airways	46,500	11,000
Northwest	53,000	10,000
America West	14,000	2,000
Midway (halted all operations on September 12)	1,900	1,700
American Trans Air	8,000	1,500
Spirit	2,400	800
Mesa Air	4,000	700
Midwest Express	3,750	450
Frontier	2,600	440

Boeing eliminated 20,000 to 30,000 employees in its commercial airplanes unit by the end of 2002 due to a lower number of orders for planes. Boeing delivered 538 planes during 2001. For the year 2002, Boeing originally expected to deliver between 510 and 520 aircraft, but the actual figure was in the low 400s.

Despite the major job cuts announcement, the number of layoffs was lower than the expected 100,000 due to several reasons. Thousands of employees took voluntary furloughs. In addition, more than 1,000 airline employees took an early retirement.

The Impact of September 11 on Marketing

Immediately on September 11 all U.S. airlines suspended advertising. Such a withdrawal from advertising is usually a matter of custom. After any plane crash airlines usually suspend ads for at least forty-eight hours. After the terrible events on September 11, most airlines stopped marketing for almost a month. Southwest was the exception as it started to run its advertising campaign again a week after the attacks. Then, after airlines were restarting their marketing efforts, another crash occurred. The loss of American Airlines Flight 587 in November 2001 grounded marketing efforts all over again. After this event, many marketing campaigns openly focused on safety. Safety was customers' main concern and they wanted to know what the airlines were doing to keep them safe. It was clear that getting people to fly again was the top priority for the airline industry after security issues.[8]

It became obvious that advertising campaigns could not be focused on emphasizing cheap fares, comfortable seats, or frequent-flier mileage. Before September 11, the airlines did not focus their ads on safety as many of them perceived the issue as a kind of black-cat jinx. During the year 2000, the airline industry spent $500 million on advertising. The biggest challenges, at that time, were dealing with customers who wanted to know why airlines could not adhere to the published flight schedules and why they did not make the seats in the coach section more comfortable. September 11 changed advertising significantly.

Therefore, marketing specialists started to develop strategies that airlines could use in their quest for survival. First, airlines were advised to be visible by running ads. Southwest was the exception because it had not stopped marketing efforts for the whole month as other airlines had. Southwest pulled its ads for forty-eight hours as a courtesy after the November crash in Brooklyn, but continued to run advertising immediately after that.

The second feature of the strategy was to be contrite and take responsibility instead of pointing fingers. The last feature referred to being specific. After September 11, Southwest ads were aimed at demonstrating patriotism—"Keep America Flying," while United featured ads in which real employees shared their stories. However, after the November crash, which was not caused by terrorists, the time for flag-waving was over.[9]

Different airlines used various advertising strategies. Delta hoped to get travelers back in the air by addressing their desire to connect with friends and family in a new advertising campaign. This airline referred to this as "Person to Person" ads, which featured "homesick college kids and parents traveling to see their children."[10] Delta based this marketing strategy on its belief that September 11 refocused people's energy on family and on connecting with their friends and other important parts of their lives.

United, for instance, spoke with viewers about the terrorist attacks in their television advertisements. This strategy received mixed reviews from marketing experts. Some experts suggested that even though the events of September 11 cannot be ignored, air travelers need not be reminded of these events that the industry hopes the consumers will soon forget. Saatchi and Saatchi Advertising agency wrote script, which emphasized camaraderie, passion for flying, and confidence in the company. Once the ad agency started to film the ads, it became apparent that what they said from their heart was much better than what was written.

A week after the attacks, Southwest Airlines ran a series of TV ads that demonstrated patriotism. On the other hand, American Trans developed TV ads with two fare sales without mentioning September 11.

During the spring of 2002, six months after the terrorist attacks, airlines as well as hotel chains spent large amounts of money in an attempt to get the attention of travelers. In addition, the airlines offered unusual incentives. Choice Hotels, partnered with American, United, Delta, and Northwest Airline, began a TV ad campaign. Choice Hotels includes Quality, Clarion, and Comfort brands, and is aiming at business travelers with triple airline miles for hotel stays. United Airlines, for instance, launched a marketing campaign that targeted business fliers at its Chicago hub. Moreover, Delta, Northwest, and U.S. Airways introduced a full-page print advertising that focused on leisure travelers and fares. In fact, such a heavy volume of marketing is not typical for springtime. However, in 2003 it was the best time as travelers were willing to get back in the air.[11]

The situation in the airline industry rebounded in the second half of 2002. Marketing budgets had declined even further from already being significantly down. Ad budgets were cut in order to provide a boost to the bottom line. This led to a more targeted and cost-effective strategy. As a result of a decrease in marketing budgets, airlines focused on maximizing the value of the dollars they spent. For example, Delta decided to focus spending on the hub market in Atlanta and also on Boston and New York markets. The goal of this approach is to build the market share in these three markets.[12]

The Impact of September 11 on Customer Service

Despite the fact that airlines had to deal with the terrorist attacks, employee layoffs, and an economic downturn, the major airlines managed to achieve improvements in baggage handling, on-time performance, and other aspects of customer service. In fact, all but one airline improved their scores in 2001. The following list summarizes the airline rankings based on a composite airline quality rating:

Airline	Overall Rating	Baggage Handling	On-Time Arrival
Alaska	1	1	11
US Airways	2	2	5
Northwest	3	4	4
Southwest	4	8	1
Delta	5	3	6
American	6	7	7
America West	7	5	8
Continental	8	6	3
United	9	9	9
American Eagle	10	11	10
Trans World	11	10	2

According to the experts, the economic impact of the terrorist attacks was not only a challenge, but also an opportunity for the airline industry. Improvement in on-time performance might be attributed to the enormous reduction in the number of flights. Furthermore, the amount of delays decreased by 25 percent. This is a significant improvement compared to the year 2000 when only small improvements occurred in customer service performance of U.S. airlines.

Another feature that has been added in an effort to improve customer service is the usage of e-mail, cell phones, pagers, and PDAs to inform ticket holders when flights and gates are changed. As a result, travelers can be paged when the plane is late, can do their own check-in at a self-service kiosk, or rebook a flight as well as print their own boarding pass. Many travelers do not see this service as an altruistic move by the airlines. Airlines perceived that this self-service not only saves money, but it also allows customers to control their own destiny at the airport. As customers generate their own answers to routine queries, airline representatives can move on to handling more complex issues.

Advances in wireless technology have allowed travelers to check-in via the Internet. This feature was suspended in some cases following September 11. Most major airlines also have kiosks at the airport that allow check-in. Last, but not least, frequent fliers can now book their award travel online. Previously, they could redeem the frequent flier miles online, but then they still had to call or send an e-mail to book the award.[13]

The airlines' loyalty programs and one-on-one communication have become dominant after the terrorist hijackings. In such a time of crisis, business could not be done as usual. People wanted to be updated. Therefore, sending a newsletter once a week was not enough. E-mail lists became the way to go. After the tragedy struck, loyalty programs and customer relationships became even more critical. For example, United uses an e-mail database that includes Mileage Plus loyalty members and other users registered through United.com to deliver updated information to consumers.

Another feature that airlines offer is a way to learn more about low fares for last-minute travel through subscription to weekly e-mail newsletters. Several restrictions apply to those fares. The most important restriction is that these fares are usually announced on Wednesday for departure on Saturday. The return date is limited to Monday and Tuesday. The flights are also limited to the airline's hub, so they are not available for flights to and from smaller airports.

Some airlines also developed a computer system that automatically sends apology letters to their frequent fliers. These letters are sent even before the passengers can complain about a bad experience on the flight. United Airlines' $10 million system was developed by IBM, and links the flight operations with a frequent-flier database. When a flight is canceled or delayed, a passenger list is scanned for frequent fliers and apology letters are sent automatically. This service was developed to improve customer relations. Customer service became a much higher priority after the September 11 attacks and the previous decrease in business travel. United Airlines is expecting to go even farther by giving additional compensation to disgruntled fliers depending on how upset the customer is.[14]

In addition, the airlines negotiated with the Transportation Security Administration to loosen rules regarding access to exclusive airport clubs. After September 11, business travelers' access to such clubs at the airport became very restrictive, as people had to have an airline ticket for a flight on the same day in order to be able to go there. This caused problems for many executives who used those clubs for business meetings.

Furthermore, the airlines' pricing structure was heavily criticized; many customers refered to it as irrational. In fact, the airlines have their own pricing strategy with prices varying greatly depending on who buys and when. Airlines agree that they have dozens of fares and that these fares might be different even for seats next to each other. Before the airline deregulation in 1978, the government set fares. Even though such fares were higher, they were more predictable. The current pricing system developed as a result of deregulation.

After the travel Web sites were developed, travelers became more aware of such irrationality.

The basics behind the pricing strategy are the attempt of airlines to steer demand toward the routes or days that are less popular. In addition, they want to set aside enough seats for customers who decide to travel at the last minute, who therefore have to pay the most. If they set aside too many of these seats, then the airlines will end up with empty seats that bring in no revenue. On the other hand, if they reserve too few of the seats, they have to turn away those customers who are willing to pay big bucks for the opportunity to fly. Therefore, if the plane is filling up too fast, the airlines will stop selling cheap tickets. In turn, if the plane is filling up at a slower rate than expected, the airlines will put more discount fares up for sale.[15]

In conclusion, the tragic events of September 11 as well as other variables led to the airline industry slowdown. These variables were the decline in business travel that resulted from the overall economic downturn, high costs of planes and salaries, and an increase in the price of jet fuel. Before September 11, the airline industry was already facing a full-blown crisis.

The airline industry responded to the situation after September 11 by downsizing radically, cutting flights as well as costs. Marketing strategy also changed as a result. Despite the negative consequences the airlines had to face, they managed to improve customer service.

The airline industry is already showing some signs of recovery. People are flying again, which is the most important factor. Business travel is on the way up.

Chapter 6

Advertisers and Consumer Behavior

THE NEW ECONOMY

The new economy since September 11, 2001, is affecting consumers for better or for worse. The faster the economy changes, with new innovations and opportunities, creating more choices and options for customers, the harder it is for people to be confident of what they will be earning next year and what they will be doing. The changes in the new economy have both economic and societal implications. This certainly has meaning for consumers, because although better informed and technologically astute customers can switch allegiance quickly, providing themselves with greater value and choice, providers must constantly make improvements, cut costs, add value, and create new services and products. On the societal level, as a result, people may have more economic and social stratification, but diminished time and security; less energy for family, friends, community, and self; and overall live a more frenzied existence (see Figures 6.1 and 6.2).

Various paradoxes are evident from living in the new economy. The central paradox is that most people are earning more money and living better than ever, in material terms, but growing poor in personal lives by working longer hours and working more frantically. Although the emerging economy is offering, through technology and sharpening competition between organizations, better value for consumers and great jobs for people with the right talents and skills, personal lives are acutely problematic due to the new economy. Faster economic changes that now force organizations to innovate, also have these firms develop their competitive strength on being better, faster, and cheaper than rivals. A key principle in the new economy after September 11, 2001, is that customers have more and better choices and

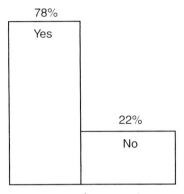

FIGURE 6.1. Percentage of organizations that face situations in which performance demands have increased since September 11, 2001 (*Source:* Carter 2003.)

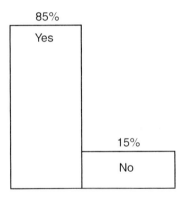

FIGURE 6.2. Percentage of managers, employees, and salespeople that feel more job stress and burnout since September 11, 2001 (*Source:* Carter 2003.)

providers are less secure and more vulnerable to competition, which is spurring innovations. The winning competitors are those who are the quickest to give lower prices, higher value, and have creative employees with good ideas. Society and organizations should focus on the realities of the new economy and how to adjust to intense competition, demanding consumers, while somehow maintaining a balance that achieves a satisfying quality of life.

ADVERTISING

The question facing advertisers is how to market to consumers who now put every aspect of their life under a microscope. The answer is very carefully. Using reports from newspapers, TV, and the Internet, studies have found that "the consumer psyche is a moving target." With the violence of September 11 looking like a movie special effect, for the advertising community, the immediate reaction was to shelve the reliance on lighthearted humor and slapstick comedy as a motif used to reel in consumers, and to be serious. Consumers and companies were not feeling very funny and the images being played around the clock on TV did not lend themselves to humor, and when the time came for humor to be used again it would have to be used sparingly.[1]

After the attack, people initially felt they would never laugh again. Consequently, ads that were deemed inappropriate were shelved or sanitized, and anything featuring airplanes, violence, and the Towers themselves were replaced. The economy pre–September 11 was already soft, and with the devastation of the number one financial center in the world, a recovery did not seem possible. Even so, the $250 billion-a-year ad industry was not centered on buying and selling commercials, but on their messages. Yet immediately after the attacks, publications issued memorial editions, some with absolutely no advertising (*Time* was one such magazine), reduced rates for memorial messages, and some magazines asked advertisers to cancel ads that were deemed inappropriate. *Fortune* magazine lost a potential $4 million and pulled more than sixty ads. Advertising for profit took a backseat to pay tribute to those who lost their lives.[2]

Advertising has long reflected the consumer's state of mind—a state of mind that changed on September 11. Consumers now felt that companies had a responsibility to support worthy causes and support their own communities. Market research also showed resurgences in patriotism, connecting with family and friends, and old-fashioned values. A study by Publicis in November 2001 asked consumers point blank what kinds of ads they wanted to see, and the majority answer was ads that were family oriented. Only a very small percent wanted to see edgy ads. Simplistic ideas and pleasures were in demand.

As a result, corporate mottos were revised to reflect the new surge in patriotism and American pride, such as Ford's "The Spirit of America," and General Motors' "Keep America Rolling." Another study by Arnold Worldwide in December 2001 surveyed 1,000 adults, and baby boomers were shown to have a new sense of nationalism—a return to the patriotic fervor of their youth.[3]

After September 11 consumers were eating more "comfort foods" with high fat content. A study by International Communications Research of Media, Pennsylvania, for GNC showed 67 percent of American resolved to enjoy their lives more. Diet and exercise, long a staple of New Years' resolutions was on the bottom of the list. Another study by the American Institute for Cancer Research showed 56 million Americans have partaken of a high fat diet since September 11. Subsequently, ads for "comfort foods," such as Kraft Macaroni & Cheese, and Nabisco Oreos remained the same. People liked the familiarity these ads possessed. Television-watching studies were also conducted; there were no dramatic shifts to one extreme or another, people had simply increased news viewership, but TV shows not mentioning the attacks or tasteless humor did increase in viewers.

It is obvious that Americans in general were changed by September 11, and ad companies used extreme sensitivity after the attacks. After all, they watched and waited too. Displaying the American flag became de rigueur for everyone—but some might have gone overboard. Many stores also changed their window displays to hang American-themed banners or dress mannequins in red, white, and blue clothing.

Advertisers that ran patriotic ads also ran the risk of becoming tasteless. How much patriotism was too much? Memorial ads were reflective, but some ads seemed to be opportunistic. An example of an ad that offended consumers was for Alamo rental cars, which used the slogan "Great American Rates" and the line "from sea to shining sea" from the National Anthem. Another ad that offended consumers was a Chrysler Jeep ad that used World War II expressions to relate to September 11. A study in 2002 by Leo Burnett USA showed that 51 percent of people polled felt companies were using patriotism for their own profit and in answer to another question, 50 percent felt it was wrong to use patriotism to encourage spending. There was obviously a fine line that was being tread during the initial burst of patriotism.[4]

Another question to ask was whether even the "good" patriotic ads would encourage spending. Would consumers purchase something simply because the company advertising it utilized patriotism? Or would the majority of consumers think it was merely opportunism? It may seem harsh to say ads are completely opportunistic and have no sentimental value, but they are just like all other aspects of the world and people—some are opportunistic and some are not. It is up to the consumer to decide which is which.

Although it is encouraging to see so many companies be patriotic, they still had to combine these messages and images with everyday life. In the February 2002 issue of the (liberal) magazine *Bad Subjects,* an essay was written by a trio of college professors (Carrie Rentschler, University of Illinois; Carol Stabile, University of Pittsburgh; and Jonathan Sterne, University of Pittsburgh) examining the patriotism-meets-capitalism phenomenon in Pittsburgh. The article's title, "United We Stand—Fresh Hoagies Daily," pretty much explains it all.

The article's authors give several examples: "In God We Trust—Huge Golf Ball Sale," Pizza Hut's "America is United, Strong and Free—Get a Job, Apply Today," a flooring company stating "Bless This Homeland Forever—Flooring Sale."[5] With ads such as these, it is easy to say that companies and businesses are being opportunistic about patriotism. On the other hand, it can be said that if we have the means to say something, even if it is something small, why shouldn't we? People can still drive by and see a phrase and be uplifted, even if they do not come in and buy something.

What marketers need to realize is that they need to show how their products can bring people together and make them feel good about being Americans, and it is not appropriate to promote greed, status, and materialism (all of which are traits that some of the world's residents see as truly American). People are leaning toward the familiar and need comfort; they do not need to dwell on the negative but rather, be uplifted.

In 2002 a study conducted for *Advertising Age* by Basking Ridge Lightspeed Research showed that marketers had not needed to change billboards or air patriotic themed ads: red, white, and blue themes made no difference to 48 percent of the 3,810 respondents, and turned away 27 percent.[6]

Although life continued to "get back to normal," the moods of consumers were still being measured as more time passed. A shift in moods has already been seen; people yearned for more than somber ads. By New Year's 2002, the American public's attitudes had changed. The Conference Board's Consumer Confidence Index was up to 93.7 as opposed to its lowest level (in October 2001) of 85.5. A poll by *The Washington Post* and ABC announced that the majority of Americans believed their country had changed for the better, and 80 percent were optimistic about the new year. Another poll by the Associated Press said that 52 percent of people expected some level of economic recovery soon.

CONSUMER BEHAVIOR

Consumer behavior has changed significantly since September 11, 2001, in terms of relationship building and emotional considerations. For example, 68 percent of executives with the 1,000 largest companies in the United States state emotional intelligence (EQ) or soft skills are more important now than ever before. Having EQ gives a 20 percent performance edge with customers.[7] EQ involves teams, motivation, persuasion, empathy, handling pressure, and satisfaction. Other emotional considerations include listening, trust, loyalty, relationship quality, understanding, and adaptability. Research suggests that listening to customers, understanding customers, and giving meaning to verbal and nonverbal and emotional messages and customer loyalty have increased in importance.

September 11 had significant effects on consumers, but they seem to be mainly personal—with priorities shifting toward family, home, and life in general. Major consumer transformations and worries about a faltering economy that were anticipated never happened. Americans decided to not give in to fear and profound sadness—life was too short.[8]

Many people are now looking for more bargains, quality, and value rather than frivolous expenditures. Some consumers are still indulging—however, a study by *Advertising Age* conducted by Ziccardi Partners Frierson Mee shows that affluent consumers are making luxury purchases for their well-being and long-lasting quality rather than as a status symbol.[9]

Although people are spending and the economy is slowly recovering, advertising continues to suffer. Company profits still are not large enough to increase ad spending—the same situation that occurred during the recession of the early 1990s. With all the studies, polls, and surveys taking place, there are conflicts—consumers are more confident, but conservative about purchases, and high levels of patriotism are still evident, though many flags have disappeared from homes, cars, and the like. Did consumers initially feel it was their patriotic duty to buy things after September 11? They had to keep the economy going, show the world that nothing, obviously not even imminent disaster, could keep them down. Missing in 2002, was a real reason to buy.[10]

The patriotic ads have also tapered off. What was initially thought to be an ongoing staple, one is hard pressed to find. Yet, if one pays attention, one would see more ads that are happier, brighter, and portraying home, family, and friendship situations.[11]

Consumers are unique, and advertisers have long tried to crack the code of consumer spending habits, ideas, and values. Given the proliferation of surveys, polls, consumer groups, and increasing demographic groups that change with the times, it is a wonder that there is no tried and true way to speak to the public. What occurred on September 11 was the best opportunity the advertising business had to understand the consumer. Americans were one big community then, not divided by sex, age, race, income, lifestyle, or hobbies.[12] Rather, we were united by a truly horrific event that attacked us as a whole—as Americans and what America represented, which was freedom and power (see Figures 6.3, 6.4, 6.5).[13]

Although initial responses were calling for a complete overhaul of every aspect of our lives, (no more violence, no more humor) things have "returned to normal," more or less, for the majority of us. We carry on with everyday life, but with new priorities and focus.[14]

It is not a matter of forgetting what happened, or even for advertisers to want to constantly remind the public, but a general, unannounced agreement by America to get on with life. The underlying message in all the ads and TV shows after September 11 is: America will survive.[15]

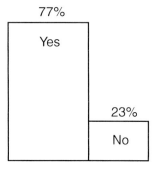

FIGURE 6.3. Percentage of organizations in which the need for customer responsiveness has increased since September 11, 2001 (*Source:* Carter 2003.)

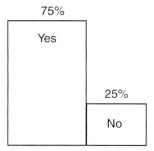

FIGURE 6.4. Managers, employees, and salespeople that feel emphasizing emotional considerations are important to customer dealings since September 11, 2001 (*Source:* Carter 2003.)

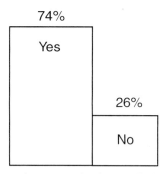

FIGURE 6.5. Managers, employees, and salespeople that feel it is more important since September 11, 2001, to understand customers more deeply (*Source:* Carter 2003.)

Chapter 7

Verizon

The most important thing a firm should do is prepare how it will handle a crisis when and if it occurs. Verizon was about to find out how prepared they were when the collapse of the World Trade Center on September 11 knocked out the Wall Street area's vital telecom service—mostly provided by Verizon. Within hours Verizon began its most important repair job to date.

Telephone service in Lower Manhattan was completely knocked out when the forty-seven-story World Trade Center Seven toppled onto a Verizon telephone center on Wall Street. The attacks had already knocked out cellular antennas and data lines, but now, a suddenly, land lines went, too, and everyone from court officials to FBI agents were scrambling to get phone service. Verizon was well aware of the urgency of reconnecting these emergency lines, and began fact gathering right away. Paul Lacouture, president of Verizon's network Service Group, and Verizon's vice chairman Larry Babbio met with New York City Mayor Rudy Giuliani to determine what telecom service the government had to have for emergency use by firemen, police, and hospitals. Verizon's first priority on the day of the attack was to reconnect communication in City Hall and 1 Police Plaza. Verizon employees began stringing lines across lampposts into 1 Police Plaza so that they could receive at least limited service. The 911 emergency service number never faltered that day because workers at Verizon began connecting 8,000 emergency lines.

Verizon also had the weight of America's economic system to worry about. The Bush Administration had insisted that the exchange open for business the Monday following the tragedy, and in less than four days Verizon had to restore 14,000 private circuits. Verizon was the stock exchange's primary telecom carrier. The exchange lost 20 percent of its phone lines and half of its data connection when Verizon's Wall Street building went out of service.

Restoring communication to the thousands of employees working in the financial district was difficult enough, but doing it in a week seemed impossible. Verizon developed certain scenarios so they would have emergency plans and processes to fall back on if something was to happen, but the amount of damage to the stock exchange would take months to restore. Verizon has a mission statement called "The Verizon Promise," which states that the core purpose of the organization is to bring about the benefit of communication to everyone and to keep their obligation to customers, communities, shareholders, and employees. This commitment to its customers was obvious when Verizon had less than a week to restore 2 million data circuits and 1.5 million phones, and all the employees did their part. Verizon accomplished the task and the trading systems that had been shut down were up and running on September 17, just six days after the attack. Investors bought and sold 2.3 billions of shares, the largest volume in the exchange's history, without a glitch.[2]

Verizon's next responsibility was to residential and business customers in the affected area. In the days after the attack the number of voice calls in the five boroughs of New York City doubled, from the normal 115 million a day to more than 230 million. For the next six days Verizon waived charges for its pay phones in Manhattan. On a single day following the disaster, residents placed some 22,000 local calls free of charge from regular sidewalk pay phones below Canal Street. Verizon met personally with public housing tenants and set up special offices for them and other residents. The company also vastly increased cell phone capacity in the damaged area and handed out cell phones with six hours of free calling to lower Manhattan customers whose lines were out. Cell phones at the time were recovering more quickly from service problems related to the disaster.

Verizon helped both big and small businesses throughout the crisis. For large customers, this meant working literally alongside them for days after the attack. It meant meeting with customers, being constantly in touch with them, monitoring their status on an hourly basis, and generally doing whatever it took to ensure the company met its commitments. Helping small businesses consisted of distributing informative flyers, setting up toll-free numbers in Spanish and Chinese, and posting information about critical services—such as call forwarding and voice mail on its Web site.[3]

Throughout the recovery effort Verizon did not wait for anyone to tell it what to do or how much it would cost. The company simply reacted and communicated the same goal to all of its customers. Verizon had one goal—to bring the lifeline of communication to everyone, and it animated the company's entire response. [4] Verizon kept consumers informed of the recovery time and provided alternatives in the meantime. Verizon also showed its commitment to customers and dedication to the recovery of the World Trade Center collapse by giving its time and money. The company held a national telethon on September 21, 2001. Thousands of employees volunteered to handle phone calls at the nine call centers that raised more than $150 million for the victims and their families. Verizon also gave several million dollars to the American Red Cross and to a benefit for the widows and children of New York City firefighters and police.

Verizon did an effective job of handling the World Trade Center crisis. Partial restoration of communications was brought about quickly after the company's switching center was damaged and its equipment went down when the World Trade Center towers collapsed. The company was able to pull together resources, people, equipment, and supplies to restore service to the New York Stock Exchange and other customers because Verizon has enough people to call upon to do work and enough equipment and supplies (such as fiber-optic cable) stockpiled to make the work possible. Verizon could have never prepared for the World Trade Center to collapse, but its readiness to handle any crisis proved very beneficial. The company was quick to react and took charge of the situation instantly. Verizon gathered facts about the situation and what needed to be done first. Verizon had backup plans set up in case something happened to the emergency communication center and that is why they were able to restore partial communications that same day. Communication was also key in how the company handled the crisis. Employees knew what was expected of them and did all they could to make sure it got done. Customers were also informed about what was being done to restore communications and were free to ask questions.

Another important aspect of preparing for a crisis is spending money, usually on technology. It takes a large amount of money to be ready for disasters, money that makes it harder to compete with other companies that might not invest the same in preparedness. Verizon spent a lot of money on equipment and backup systems that it had installed in case of a crisis and spent even more after the World Trade Center collapsed. The importance of these communications services that Verizon set up proved to be an essential part of reconnecting lower Manhattan. Custom redirect, secure managed e-mail, and remote access were critical in reconnecting hundreds of displaced employees and allowing them to work from alternate sites.[5]

SALES ORGANIZATIONAL COMMUNICATION

Before the World Trade Center collapse Verizon found itself having communication problems between its sales managers and subordinates. Communication, which was such an important part of the recovery effort, was missing within the organization and causing problems. Problems arise when sales managers believe they communicate more effectively than they do or subordinates believe these managers are more open to communication than they actually are. During Verizon's eighteen-day strike in 2003, many employees expressed that a companywide values statement clashed with reality in the area of customer service. The core values in Verizon's statement are integrity, respect, imagination, passion, and service. Many of Verizon's customer service representatives feel that the company's core beliefs are contradicted by the fact that they have to read scripts. The problem with the script is that the representative does not sound natural and does not project concern for the consumer. The script was meant to be a management tool of measurement—a way to promote better and more measurable service and sales—but employees feel completely disconnected to this effort. Sales representatives do not trust sales managers who ask them to use their imagination while handing them a script. Sales managers can overcome employee distrust by empowering the sales force, being supportive, open, and actively listening.[6]

Job Stress

At the heart of this strike between Verizon and its telecommunications workers were the high stress levels experienced by sales representatives. Job burnout occurs after prolonged periods of unrelenting stress on the job. The eighteen-day strike by telephone workers against

Verizon was motivated in large part by overtime issues; women in the company's calling system complained that they could not break free from work early enough to pick up their children or make dinner for their families. As worker burnout became more common, the need to have forced overtime became a problem. Major problems that lead to job burnout have been identified as:

1. *Poor supervision, including a supervisor who is critical, expects too much, is not open to discussing problems, organizes departmental work poorly, and does not recognize employees for a job well done.* Poor supervision often occurred during "observation." One major cause of stress for many representatives is this so called "observation," which occurs routinely when a manager sits next to a representative or listens in on a call to check whether he or she has hit on nearly eighty different points required in every customer contact. During this time a representative may get extremely nervous, especially someone who is new to the job and has just missed the essential six-point greeting and eight points related to selling Verizon products and services. Many sales representatives also felt that supervisors expect too much of them and are too critical. Many complained about the presence of a "force manager," whose job was to make sure that a call center was running at peak efficiency and traced various call center vital signs on a computer.

2. *Lack of teamwork, including tension and feelings with a group and failure to pitch in when needed.* Sales representatives felt that they were being asked to do too much without much help from management. Representatives are given monthly sales objectives, and are expected to offer services as caller ID, call waiting, and DSL Internet access.[7]

3. *Unreasonable workload, including employees who feel overworked, cannot meet deadlines, and cannot keep up with changes.* Sales representatives at Verizon had to adhere to strict standards, such as keeping a phone line open to receive calls 92 percent of the workday and keeping customers on hold for no more than two minutes at a time. If these standards were not met it could lead to probation, suspension, and termination, or what the company refers to as "separation from payroll." Sales repre-

sentatives were also required to focus on selling new products rather than just answering consumer complaints and offering service.[8]

4. *Unfair company practices, including promotions that are perceived as unjust and discrimination on the basis of race, sex, or age.* Verizon wanted to limit to 1.5 percent the number of workers that can transfer each month. This would trap customer service representatives and consultants in high-pressure jobs without opportunities for movement.[9]

In 2003 Verizon finally came to an agreement with the Communications Workers of America. The new contract states that a representative's overall performance rating can no longer be tied to sales performance. Representatives will also be guaranteed fifteen minutes off the phone each day and another fifteen minutes so that they can complete paperwork at their desks.[10] Verizon also boosted its training program and now offers flextime. The new contract also states that reps can only work 7.5 hours of overtime per week and that managers are required to give prior notice of an observation on the day it is to occur.

Chapter 8

Aon

INTRODUCTION

On September 11, 2001, lives in the United States would be changed forever when four hijacked planes took Americans' feelings of security and invincibility away. This was confirmed with planes hitting and destroying the World Trade Center and partially damaging the Pentagon. The last hijacked plane, which departed from Newark, New Jersey, crashed in rural Somerset County, Pennsylvania. This day of infamy demonstrated America's vulnerability to terrorist attacks. These attacks brought about an unprecedented stoppage of U.S. air travel and closure of all U.S. stock exchanges. Suddenly, bomb scares and bridge and tunnel closures became regular occurrences in New York City and across the nation. Nearly 3,000 civilians lost their lives due to this act, with the brunt of the losses in New York. Although this act of terror replaced the feeling of security with fear, Americans and New Yorkers especially showed resilience by going on with their daily lives. In the face of adversity, Americans responded with courage and determination, and above all, unity.[1]

The World Trade Center was a symbol of America's power and capitalism. The twin towers were dedicated in 1973 and quickly became the symbol of New York and American icons. The World Trade Center complex consisted of Tower One (north) and Tower Two (south) and numerous smaller buildings. The twin towers were now the most recognizable buildings in New York, and the World Trade Center was deemed the financial capital of the world. The World Trade Center Complex, owned by the Port Authority of New York and New Jersey, housed 500 businesses with approximately 50,000 employees. This office space included brokerage firms, airlines, television stations, banks, law firms, chapels of various faiths, and an underground shopping mall. On an average day nearly 200,000 visitors from all over the world visited the complex. This made the World Trade Center a lucrative site to cause mass destruction.[2]

THE 1993 WORLD TRADE CENTER BOMBING

An unsuccessful bombing in 1993 was attempted but minimal damage was obtained. The World Trade Center was a major artery for public transportation flowing through it such as the PATH and various other New York City subways. The World Trade Center's large antenna atop the building one roof was used as a transmitter for television, cellular phone service, and radio broadcasting. After the towers collapsed, telephone communication into the city was nearly impossible. This building was more than a fixture in New York's beautiful skyline—it was the heart of New York, which many industries flowed through. Unlike the blast in 1993, the World Trade Center succumbed on September 11, 2001, and Tower One and Tower Two collapsed. These collapsed buildings marked a change in the way most Americans lived. No longer could we walk around with blinders on.

THE SEPTEMBER 11 ATTACKS

Economic Consequences

The World Trade Center attack not only caused enormous loss of life, previously it sent an already depressed economy to rock bottom. As stated, the World Trade Center was the heart of downtown Manhattan—when the towers collapsed so did the businesses that thrived in and around the World Trade Center. New York City's economy lost an estimated 108,500 jobs as a direct result of the attack. These terrorist attacks cost New York $16.9 billion dollars. The goal of these attacks was to put terror in the hearts of Americans and to hit the United States at the center of its economy. The securities industry, retail, and restaurants were severely affected. Numerous businesses were destroyed or forced to close. Many of these surrounding businesses depended on tourists from the World Trade Center to support their businesses, which caused many firms to cut their staffs.[3]

Aon Corporation

Aon Corporation was hit hard by the World Trade Center attacks. Even though insurance carriers had minimal job losses they suffered tremendously with claims and brought about coverage issues that the government is examining and debating.

Aon Corporation, a Fortune 500 business headquartered in Chicago, Illinois, is a holding company that consists of insurance brokerage, consulting, and insurance underwriting subsidiaries. Aon Corporation is a global firm that dominates many sectors of the industry. Aon is the world's:

- No. 1 global reinsurance broker
- No. 1 global manager of captive insurance companies
- No. 1 U.S. multiline claims services provider
- No. 1 U.S. wholesale broker and underwriting manager
- No. 2 global insurance broker
- No. 6 employee benefits consultant

Aon has approximately 53,000 employees worldwide with 550 offices in more than 125 countries. Aon's business structure consists of seven major divisions:

- Aon Consulting
- Aon Re Worldwide
- Aon Risk Services
- Aon Services Group
- Aon Warranty Group
- Combined Insurance
- Virginia Surety Company/London General Insurance

Within these divisions Aon performs services dealing with employees benefits; compensation; management consulting; risk management; and supplemental accident, health, and life insurance. In most of these divisions Aon is clearly a global leader in the industry, second only to Marsh & McLennan.[4]

Shortly after 1993 Aon moved its offices into Two World Trade Center alongside its major competitor Marsh & McLennan. The firm occupied nine floors, 92 and 98 to 105, with approximately 1,100 employees in the New York hub. These floors were the worst places to be relative to the impact zone. Many people were left trapped with no alternative but to jump or be burned alive. Aon was hit very hard by the attacks as many people chose their fate immediately after the first plane hit Tower One. Those who chose to leave against building announcements were ultimately saved; those who did not lost their lives. Aon lost nearly 200 employees to this senseless act of violence. Many employees, as with the rest of the nation, were left traumatized by the experience of this terrible event.

How did Aon handle this difficult situation in the aftermath of the attacks? It recognized that the company had a full-fledged crisis on its hands. A crisis is defined as a major unpredictable event that has potentially negative results. These terrorist attacks on the World Trade Center definitely could be classified as unpredictable and had definite negative results. Even though Aon specializes in risk services and management, this event was completely unpredictable and never could be imagined even in anyone's wildest dreams. A crisis can be a turning point in any firm. It can affect sales, employee morale, operating expenses, and financial conditions. Aon had to act fast as did most other firms in this tragedy, to ensure its survival as as corporation and to handle this delicate situation with the utmost care. Even in the wake of disaster public relations is extremely important; no corporation wants bad press and backlash from surviving employees about how insensitively the company reacted. It was a tremendous help that Aon had a crisis management practice that was founded in 1999 to assist it in this difficult process. Crisis management is not only about predicting that things will go wrong, but developing a plan of action once the crisis has occurred. The Framework for Crisis Solutions was exhibited by Aon. The first step, fact gathering, consisted of locating employees' whereabouts. The crisis management team quickly established a hotline and command center to account for all employees, stating that employee safety was their primary focus. Communicating the message was widely used by the crisis management team. The team relayed information to its customers, employees, and shareholders. Crisis centers were established to counsel many employees who lost co-workers and provide psychological help in understanding why this violent attack occurred. Crisis management teams were focused on employee morale, giving employees ample time to grieve. Employees were asked to come back to work after three weeks, and if more time was needed it was granted. After September, memorials were held at St. Patrick's Cathedral as well as a meeting at the Waldorf-Astoria to promote unity and show that a support network existed within the company. Salaries were continued for all employees until relocation could be achieved. Salaries were also continued for deceased employees for six weeks. Office space was finally found in midtown Manhattan three weeks after the attack. Learning from the events of September 11, Aon teamed up with former New York City mayor Rudy Giuliani to provide corporate crisis management. Giuliani Partners LLC and Aon formed a strategic alliance to provide crisis management services to major corporations around the world. Giuliani states, "I learned all the time when I was mayor of New York City that the best answer to a crisis is relentless preparation."[5] This alliance with Giuliani and his former staffers will provide firms with short-term and long-term crisis management solutions, aid in the development and implementation of comprehensive crisis operations protocols, and advice on internal and external emergency communications procedures. Giuliani led New York City through its crisis and is now applying his skills with Aon. Both sides recognize the need to be prepared. Aon CEO Patrick Ryan states that "Companies today must prepare for what was previously inconceivable. Merging our expertise with that of Rudy Giuliani, whose leadership skills have set a crisis management standard for the world, made perfect sense."[6] As discussed previously, Aon already had a global crisis management team and drew from that experience. Aon also created in 1997 a special risks counterterrorism team, which combines military and insurance experience to provide risk transfer and risk management solutions to clients who are exposed to terrorism. It also has developed risk management and insurance solutions in the event that chemical, radiological, and biological warfare are used. These are issues that most Americans never envisioned worrying about here on U.S. soil, but these are issues that firms need to consider to bring quality service to consumers and to protect employees and the firm's assets.[7]

Every firm must plan for business continuity across all industries. Many firms post–September 11 are scrambling to refine their business continuity programs. Business continuity is being prepared in case something happens to the home office, usually in the event of a fire or natural disaster. Now firms must prepare for terrorist attacks as well. Many of Aon's clients are expressing a desire to enhance resumption planning, security, and evacuation planning provisions. Business continuity has been thought of in the past as a waste of time by many, but now it has become a way of life. After the attack on the World Trade Center, Aon's client servicing was rerouted to its client service business units in Los Angeles, Houston, and Illinois. Aon was still able to manage quality customer service throughout the whole ordeal until its New York office relocated. All of the data files that were contained in the World Trade Center were backed up at the Chicago headquarters as well as the Houston office. This practice is common and ensures that service will not be interrupted to clients. The only addition to business continuity would be to practice evacuation routines in the event of a fire, bombing, or biological warfare. So, in the event that disaster strikes again people will be evacuated immediately, not taking anything for granted. America must be ready for anything at anytime.[8]

Reengineering is defined as altering existing models and thinking. Internal and external changes in the environment may warrant a need to do things differently. These changes can consist of technological advances, globalization, and catastrophic business crises. In the case of the September 11 attacks, Aon's reengineering process focused on catastrophic business crises. As the insurance industry is changing, Aon's services in terms of insurance coverage and risk management will be needed more than ever. Aon began its reengineering process by hiring Rudy Giuliani and his firm to assist its crisis management area with public safety, emergency preparedness, and leadership during crisis. In 2004 and beyond, this is what clients will need, and Aon must find a better way to give customers what they want. By incorporating these strategies Aon will have a competitive advantage and increase revenue. Aon is also using reengineering to boost morale for employees. Aon knows that in the coming years preserving the memory of their co-workers will be paramount in employees' minds. Aon has founded the Aon Memorial Education Fund to honor the memories of fallen colleagues. The fund was created so that victims' children could pursue collegiate endeavors. In 2003, many employees ran in the New York City and Chicago marathons to raise funds and also to help raise awareness to the cause. With these charitable programs, it has helped employees heal and has shown that Aon has not abandoned the people who have worked so hard for it over the years. This is the type of reengineering that is needed to bring unity within the firm.[9]

Aon was hit hard financially by the attacks on the World Trade Center. Aon's Combined Insurance Company had to pay $45 million in insurance benefits to employees. They also extended medical benefits of $7 million to the families of deceased employees. Insurance claims are still being processed relating to losses that Aon suffered and how much it really costs them in terms of business interruption is still unknown. Last, the cost of finding interim office space for the year after the disaster must also be factored in. This is just another example of how all firms have changed the way they do business. Unfortunately all this hardship has not faded. Aon is still struggling to regain itself in the wake of September 11 and a SEC probe into its accounting practices.

The insurance industry as a whole was hit extremely hard by the events of September 11, and is still reeling from the attacks. The issue of insuring against terrorist attacks is causing debate within Congress and the industry itself. Insurance companies across the board are still trying to quantify the exact loss suffered. It is estimated that anywhere between $40 to $70 billion was lost. The big debate with insurance companies today is whether these terrorist attacks were an act of war. If the attacks were classified that way many insurance carriers could deny coverage. Most insurance contracts contain war exclusions, such as:

- war (declared or undeclared),
- civil war,
- military action,
- insurrection,
- rebellion, and
- revolution.

Another avenue that is being questioned by insurers is the "one or two occurrence" debate. The Port Authority wants to classify the attacks as two occurrences so they will be covered for both towers and paid accordingly as if it were two separate instances. The insurers believe that it was one occurrence. The only flip side to denying cover-

age is the bad public relations that will follow. American patriotism is
at an all-time high—if insurance companies start denying claims they
could lose a substantial amount of revenue. The American public at
this point in time will not support firms that are not putting the needs
of the country and its people first at this critical time. Companies do
not want to be the firm known for not paying claims to innocent victims of the tragedy and their families. This leaves the industry in a
tough spot. The industry has already stated that it cannot financially
handle another major terrorist attack. These circumstances have prompted the government to examine the situation a little further. President
Bush is urging Congress to adopt legislation to protect the insurance
industry from losses due to future terrorists attacks. It is the House
and the Senate's objective to make terrorism insurance widely available at affordable prices, thus limiting the liability of the insurance industry. Congress is extremely close to finalizing a deal to provide up
to $100 billion of support to the insurance industry in the event of a
future terrorist attack.[10] The general deal involves the government
paying 80 percent of losses up to $10 billion and 90 percent above
that. The other suggestion proposed by the House gives the secretary
of commerce discretion to decide whether to actually require the insurers to pay back loans or leave the costs to be paid by taxpayers.[11]
The flip side of bailing out the insurance industry is that it would reduce the industry's incentive to require clients to take adequate security measures that would deter terrorists. If the government is backing
them up to a certain percentage, insurance companies will only be lia-
ble to a limit.[12] These issues are still being heavily debated, but it is
clear that President Bush is committed to putting this through as legislation. This would give him enormous credit and could define his
presidency. President Bush is also thinking about reelection and how
he handled the aftermath of September 11 is paramount in the American public's mind.[13]

The insurance industry is also being plagued by a sluggish U.S.
stock market. Poor underwriting in 2001 cost the industry $27 billion
in capital. The industry lost so much revenue because it no longer
could depend on attractive investment yields, which would cover the
cost of underpriced premiums. With a lagging market, increased
claims, terrorism coverage, and poor underwriting, this industry must
come up with new and innovative plans to keep up with these challenging times.[14]

Chapter 9

PricewaterhouseCoopers

OVERVIEW

The attacks on September 11, 2001, have had a far-reaching impact on American businesses. Economists who predict and study business trends analyzed data comparing the state of the economy prior to September 11 to the months that followed the attack. According to an article in *The Washington Post,* the U.S. economy, which was already weakening in the summer of 2001, ground to a virtual halt in mid-September. Many businesses ceased functioning, theaters went empty, airlines stopped flying, advertisements were pulled, and the Dow Jones industrial average plunged nearly 685 points.

Due to quick action by the federal government and lower interest rates, American consumers were eased back into a familiar spending pattern with the housing industry and the automobile industry leading the way. According to Paul Bluestein of *The Washington Post,* the economy surged at a 6 percent annual rate in the fourth quarter in 2001. CEOs of America's fastest growing companies had to revise their strategies and restructure their businesses in terms of crisis management, revenue growth, forecasting/restructuring business strategy, client loyalty, and the targeting of new clients. Managers at PricewaterhouseCoopers LLP (PwC) experienced and were involved with internal planning and restructuring in the aftermath of September 11 in terms of crisis management, restructuring business strategy/reforecasting revenue growth, and client service. They also saw the impact of September 11 on PwC's clients in terms of the same three business areas.

No one can be completely prepared for the many challenges that an unexpected crisis can cause. An individual who loses his or her job or suffers a major illness faces economic and psychological hardships that can often deplete his or her resources. Businesses, as with individuals, often face the same consequence as a result of major unpredictable events. The major difference is that businesses often have more resources to meet the potentially negative issues of a crisis. This planning of strategy is the function of a crisis management team in an organization. Managers must wrestle with the challenges of post-attack workplaces by reassuring nervous workers, increasing productivity, and coping with a new reality. In an article in *USA TODAY* more than 30 percent of American workers were fearful of entering their workplace, traveling on business, and being exposed to an anthrax attack.[1]

At PwC, leadership faced the same challenges mentioned earlier. The first difficulty that PwC's crisis management team began to work on was to improve the firm's capability to respond to emergencies. One of the vital lessons the firm learned from the tragedy was the importance of maintaining contact and the ability to communicate with PwC employees. As part of the effort, the firm launched an emergency hotline, which can be reached twenty-four hours a day through a toll-free number. The hotline is a means for employees to obtain information should a serious emergency situation arise. It is also a way that employees can stay in touch with the firm. Families and friends also have access to hotline staff so that communication can be maintained. In addition to current updates on a particular crisis, the hotline staff has the capability of receiving information and handling inquiries. In a crisis an employee can call the hotline to give his or her location and health status. At the same time an employee's family member can receive the exact information. This organization of information has served to calm many employees and their families, especially in cases where employees have frequent travel needs. The emergency hotline is staffed at all times and is fully activated in a crisis situation. A special team of human resource professionals will call emergency contacts and talk to concerned family members during a crisis. The human resources team is fully trained and has participated in drills to test and refine the process. They have conducted information sessions with various groups of employees at all levels to apprise them of the services available through the hotline. The feedback that they have received has been extremely positive. Employees have stated that they are less apprehensive about travel and feel more confident that information will be disseminated properly.[2]

Although the hotline service has been effective, the management at PwC felt the necessity to take additional steps to meet the challenges of dealing with the aftermath of September 11. The metropolitan division of the firm lost five employees in the terrorist attacks and provided counseling to families and co-workers. The firm hired professional counselors who met with employees in groups and individually. Counselors were also available to the family members of employees who lost their lives in the tragedy. Counseling services were available twenty-four hours a day. Employees were also encouraged to submit their feelings electronically on a special Web site created after the tragedy. Crisis counseling was also available to those employees who were alarmed by a growing dependency on drugs or alcohol. In addition, PwC partners contributed over $1 million from their personal funds to assist the family members of employees who lost their lives in the tragedy. Managers and members of the crisis management team became involved with PwC's legal department in order to facilitate the distribution of emergency financial funds to the families of affected personnel. Crisis management legal seminars were conducted that deal with the legal ramifications of the distribution of emergency funds. Another feature of the seminar, which is critical to crisis management, concerned the issue of employer negligence with respect to improper procedures and planning for crisis. The seminar also included topics concerning employee background checks, how to conduct investigations, and how to detect the warning signs of potentially volatile employee behavior. The legal seminar also included topics concerning the special needs of employees with disabilities, particularly during evacuation due to a crisis situation. The crisis management team is responsible for informing colleagues of what was covered in the seminar.[3]

Safety concerns became more of an issue in the aftermath of September 11. Managers have had to lead employees who must work amid bomb threats, anthrax scares, terrorist attack warnings, and building evacuations. PwC has had to face similar safety concerns. The crisis management team had to develop an action plan to deal with these issues. In order to cope with a difficult security issue the team developed a new photo identification policy, requiring all PwC employees to wear identification badges. Security personnel were also increased at all offices in the New York City metro area. Building evacuation plans were revised and drilled routinely. PwC focused on ensuring that all employee emergency contact information was updated and accurate, and was responsible for communicating the new policies to employees and for the enforcement of these policies.

PWC'S CUSTOMERS

Verizon Wireless

Nearly half of the CEOs at the nation's fastest-growing companies (47 percent) say it was more difficult to develop a budget for their business this year, compared to a year ago, because of economic volatility due to the aftermath of September 11. Research shows a 5.8 percent increase in their budget for previously unexpected new expenditures was for issues relating to security and safety. One of PwC's clients, Verizon Wireless, faced this situation with respect to an increase in budget relating to crisis management issues. The Lower Manhattan location of Verizon Wireless' facilities and the nature of its business made it vulnerable to crisis and security issues. Verizon Wireless is in the business of communication services. Any major, unpredictable event can cause disastrous effects for a company such as Verizon Wireless. Catastrophic losses in equipment, personnel, and material can affect the virtual survival of a corporation. According to Verizon Wireless executive Robert Yatwa, the security budget for the New Jersey facilities in 2003 "increased over one hundred thousand dollars monthly." [4] This involved the installation of checkpoints associated with security stations, parking facility patrols, increased electronic surveillance, and preregistration for all visitors at the New Jersey facilities. One of the new procedures instituted at the New Jersey facilities paralleled PwC's emergency hotline program.

The focus of the emergency hotline program at Verizon Wireless accommodates a great number of employees who do not operate out of a central location. The ability to get information to these employees who work in the field becomes more critical and complicated. An additional problem arises when this information needs to be centralized and communicated to the families of employees. To solve these issues intermediate stations and information centers were created. Another feature of the company's emergency plan involves business continuation strategies and contingency planning. For example, if a site experiences a complete shutdown, a backup site is activated to compensate. To accomplish this, an emphasis to create new backup sites around the metropolitan area became an important focus for Verizon Wireless. The funding for these new procedures involved transferring capital from a previously planned network expansion program and a heavy reliance on loans from the parent company, Verizon.[5]

Interviews of CEOs at America's fastest-growing companies show that shortly after the September 11 terrorist attacks two sharply differing perspectives on the future growth of their businesses emerged. CEOs contacted in August and early September 2001 projected a modest improvement in their growth over the next year. However, those interviewed in late September and early October 2001 anticipated revenue growth 22 percent lower, with plans for business investments and new hiring similarly affected. Most senior executives (73 percent) in a broad spectrum of multinational companies said that the September 11 attacks had negatively impacted their business and that they had scaled back already-reduced growth estimates by an additional 10 percent. PwC also needed to reforecast its expected revenue growth budget. September 11 greatly affected many of PwC's clients and in turn its own business. Client executives, leery of the possibility of another attack and the poor economy, were suddenly not as willing to take on projects that would cost their companies thousands of dollars up front. PwC reported negative results for the September through December 2001 time period. The firm's partners were unable to keep many of their employees busy with client work and projects. In response to the crisis, PwC placed a strict hiring freeze for all open positions within the firm and focused on cost-cutting procedures. Travel was restricted unless absolutely necessary. Leadership charged human resources with the task of developing other significant methods to reduce cost. The human resources team was involved in creating a cost containment plan for the New York City metropolitan area. The plan called for human resources representatives to work closely with the finance department to monitor client billing and receivables. If a client was not being billed for services rendered in a timely fashion, a member of human resources would contact the billing partner and/or manager to ensure that the services would be billed for and collected. A new focus was also placed on reviewing employee expense reports and enforcing the firm's reimbursement policies. Over the course of a year the human resource team was able to save the company hundreds of thousands of dollars in the metro region and millions of dollars nationwide.[6]

PwC leadership realized that, after September 11, companies would need to concentrate internally on their own people and businesses. PwC clients such as Verizon Wireless, Agere, and Avaya all reported net losses of hundreds of millions of dollars for their respective businesses during the final quarter of fiscal year 2001. In Verizon Wireless' case, according to Mr. Yatwa, due to the fact that the network expansion project was delayed, because the planned funding for the project was needed to increase security and improve emergency contingency planning the business strategy at Verizon Wireless which involved the targeting of new cellular phone customers had to be revised downward. In addition to these unexpected expenditures on security, cell phone usage dropped after September 11 fueled by the loss of jobs and the general downward economic trend. In addition, Verizon Wireless had to spend a great deal of money getting its service back up and running to full capacity after the collapse of the World Trade Center towers, which housed much of its communication technology. In summary, what did this mean to Verizon Wireless? According to Mr. Yatwa, "Rival cellular phone companies closed the gap with respect to new business, and service."[7]

Agere Systems

In an October 2001 press release, Agere Systems, one of the largest providers of components for communication applications, announced that its revenue for the fourth quarter ending in September 2001 was down approximately 35 percent. The company also announced in December of the same year its plans to eliminate 6,000 jobs as a broad restructuring of its workforce. Agere is implementing the restructure to align its business with current market conditions. According to Agere CEO John Dickson the company needs to reduce its workforce and cut costs to survive. In the December press release Mr. Dickson is quoted as saying, "It is critical that we continue to move forward with our plans to lower our cost structure and direct our resources to areas that will best support our return to profitable growth." Mr. Dickson also states in the same interview that 2001 was an extremely difficult year for Agere's business, it customers, and its people. According to Kim Smith, the technology tax specialist at PWC, "The technology sector was already feeling the downward trend in the economy. September 11 amplified the need for technology and communications companies to retool their objectives and business strategies or be hit with continued negative results."[8]

Avaya Inc.

Avaya Inc., a leading global provider of corporate communications networking solutions and services, also reported a decrease of 29.2 percent or $596 million compared to revenues from ongoing operations of a year.[9] The company also noted that in the fourth quarter of 2001, virtually all business segments around the world were affected by an industry-wide slowdown. Company executives had to develop a restructuring plan to work more efficiently and effectively. Avaya decreased its workforce and increased its focus in research and development for the next generation of communications products and applications. The restructuring plan positioned Avaya to better serve the needs of customers, which, according to company executives, should cause revenue to grow when the economy begins to improve. The restructuring plan also included the aggressive management of expenses not associated with research and development. It is also part of Avaya's plan to maintain fiscal management on an expense-to-revenue basis.

To any business the importance of being customer driven and service oriented is magnified after an event such as September 11. It is key for companies that wish to remain successful to realize that with crisis comes opportunity. Successful companies focus on improving the quality of customer services while meeting the additional needs created by a crisis. PwC, Agere, and Avaya successfully put into place a plan to accomplish the objective of meeting the changing needs of its clients in the aftermath of the September 11 attacks.[10]

PwC took the approach of allowing clients who were most affected by the tragedy to delay paying bills for work performed. PwC also started a campaign of contacting clients, not with the intent to sell new work, but with asking clients how PwC can help them. Because PwC focuses on the taxation concerns of companies, the firm had to develop new strategies to assist its clients to cope with meeting its tax requirements. One must keep in mind that PwC had to accomplish this objective during a downward trend in the economy. PwC's clients were faced with new tax laws and a reduction in profits. PwC was successful with helping clients obtain filing extensions and to take advantage of the new tax laws that were created to assist companies affected by the September 11 tragedy. PwC's tax specialists researched the new tax disaster relief laws and invited clients, as well as prospective clients, to instructional workshops that focused on how these laws could be advantageous to a company. The tax specialists took this process a step further. Not all tax relief laws applied to every company in the same way. The key element for the specialists was tailoring the information to the specific needs of different companies. This required meticulous work and preparation to alter the focus of the workshops in order to help clients obtain tax relief in a critical time in their operations. After the effects of the tragedy subsided, many clients were grateful for PwC's focused efforts.

Avaya also needed to develop new strategies for improvement in customer services. Avaya announced a customer relationship management (CRM) alliance to assist enterprises in increasing operational efficiency, enhancing/retaining customer relations, and supporting revenue growth. One of the many features of the CRM alliance is the interaction center that Avaya introduced. The interaction center is a software program that enables businesses to add communications channels such as e-mail, voice, Web chat, and browser-based collaboration to multivendor networks. The software ties all of these networks together into a single administration. The company also introduced Avaya Speech Access for Unified Messenger, the first unified messaging program that allows mobile workers to access voice messaging and other functions, such as e-mail, with natural conversation from any phone. This gives a growing mobile workforce access to critical communication tools using simple voice commands.

Avaya also introduced an enhanced surety application for its virtual private networks that addresses the most challenging wireless local area network security requirements. This feature is particularly important in today's business environment to prevent hackers from infiltrating computer systems. The entire CRM program introduced by Avaya not only improved customer service, but restored much needed confidence to the business community that Avaya services. Avaya's clients depend upon secure and expeditious communications to execute their day-to-day business needs and to give access to workers and clients. According to market research, the CRM program will yield an annual growth rate of 25.2 percent in new business and is expected to surpass $148 billion in revenue growth by 2005.[11]

CONCLUSION

Companies such as PwC, Verizon Wireless, Avaya, and Agere began to lower their forecasted growth budgets and revise their business plans. This called for a reduction in their respective workforces, cost containment strategies, restructuring of their organizations, and an increased focus on customer research and service. In the aftermath of September 11, companies had to do more with less. In addition to all of these concerns, these companies had to contend with an extremely nervous and frightened workforce who were not only worried about their jobs, but were also concerned for their personal safety at the work site. Executives needed to become crisis managers, planning for events over which they virtually had no control. Managers needed to think in innovative ways to combat the psychological effects of an event such as the September 11 attacks. The suddenness of this event made this situation different for managers even though they have faced downward trends in business before. In a recession, which is sometimes cyclical and often predictable, business managers can rely upon many indicators to help forecast the downward economic trend. A recession, therefore, is gradual, enabling a business enterprise to prepare to meet its challenges in terms of employment, revenue growth, crisis management, and customer relations. A terrorist attack such as occurred on September 11 had immediate macroeconomic effects on a global scale, similar in many ways to the stock market crash of 1929. The crash of 1929 fired the shot that began a worldwide depression that lasted for more than ten years. Although the economy remains volatile today, due to the strategic thinking, planning, and action of today's business leaders, enterprises will be able to avoid the tragedies of another worldwide depression.[12]

Chapter 10

A Global Examination
of International Marketing

INTRODUCTION

September 11, better known as 9/11, was this generation's Pearl Harbor. An unspeakable evil perpetrated for what seems to be no rational reasoning. The people who died September 11 were not soldiers. There was no inherent risk in being a stockbroker or a waiter or an insurance agent. These people arose with simple agendas, go to work, take a flight, handle business, have some fun. They were not supposed to be attacked by rogue factions bent on changing what they believe is an evil world. Being Americans in America was never supposed to be dangerous. This is the land of the free and the brave—the land of democracy, free speech, freedom of the press, and freedom of religion. In many ways on September 11 the hijackers of those four flights managed to alter that.[1]

INTERNATIONAL MARKETING

International marketing is defined as "the performance of business activities designed to plan, price, promote, and direct the flow of a company's goods and services to consumers or users in more than one nation for a profit."[2] In this day and age, no country has the ability to stand on its own. Commerce and money are the international languages that forge diplomacy and foreign relations. Current interest in international marketing can be explained by changing competitive structures coupled with shifts in demand characteristics in markets throughout the world. In current business practices a company will face rivals in both domestic and international circles. There is no clear front on which to fight. "With the increasing globalization of markets, companies find they are unavoidably enmeshed with foreign customers, competitors and suppliers, even within their own borders."[3] For large corporations to be successful in this day and age they need to be global.

International Marketing and World Peace

> Global commerce thrives during peacetime. The economic boom of the late 1990s was in large part due to the end of the Cold War and the opening of the formerly communist countries to the world trading systems. However, we should also understand the important role that trade and international marketing play in actually producing world peace.[4]

This passage was authored before September 11, 2001.

Successful International Marketing

The task of picking a target market is no small endeavor. A great deal of forethought and work must be done to successfully breach, integrate, and assimilate into foreign markets. Companies that do not spend the time on research and developing *global marketing plans* will not succeed.

The first thing that has to be examined is a country's infrastructure; another point of interest is its legal code. Three main types of legal code exist. The first is common law, which is used in the United States and England. The second is code law, which is used in countries such as Poland and France. The third is Islamic law, which is used in Middle Eastern Islamic countries. All three are different and need to be understood.

Cultures and customs need to be understood before entering target markets. Different aspects of society are valued more and less in cultures that differ from the United States. Understanding these cultures, and adapting with the realization that there is no right or wrong way to do things, and that every culture differs is the strongest way to build solid relationships.[5]

Big Emerging Markets

Big emerging markets, more commonly referred to as BEMs, are areas that have vast potential because of good natural resources and or abundant markets that are prime for developing. The two most promising markets in today's financial world are China and Poland. China is the largest emerging market in the world with an estimated 2 billion consumers. Poland is the largest emerging market in Europe. Both have vast potential. Companies worldwide must direct attention to both of these markets, especially China with such an incredible population, in order to be truly global companies. However, with the threat of terrorism and war around the globe, especially with the terrorist attacks in Bali and Saudi Arabia, concerns are raised that international trade and all countries and companies involved will suffer.

Organizations Protecting International Marketing

The International Marketing Supervision Network (IMSN) is a membership organization consisting of the trade practices law enforcement authorities of more than two dozen countries, most of which are members of the Organisation for Economic Co-operation and Development (OECD). IMSN's mandate is to share information about cross-border commercial activities that may affect consumer interests, and to encourage international cooperation among law enforcement agencies. The IMSN operates under a rotating presidency, currently held by Australia. The working languages of the IMSN are French and English.

The IMSN is one of many agencies that concern themselves with the successful advancement of international trade and marketing. Its member countries include the United States, the United Kingdom, and Japan to name three of twenty-nine; members of the European Union are also involved. The IMSN operates an informal dispute resolution system to assist consumers in resolving disputes arising from cross-border transactions.

INTERNATIONAL MARKETING CONCERNS POST–SEPTEMBER 11

In an article published September 18, 2001, Maria Livanos Cattaui asserted that business needed to continue in the wake of the September 11 attacks, not "as usual" but rather "business despite what happened."[6] This attitude is essential because there needs to be mourning and remembrance for the catastrophic loss of life. However, if we allow the financial world to crumble then the terrorists have taken more than just life.

> They [terrorists] want to push the world economy into recession. If their actions have demonstrably inflicted severe injury, however temporary, on capitalism, they will exult. If they feel that they have stopped global economic integration in its tracks, they will rejoice. Those rewards must be denied them. That is the least the worldwide business community can do for the victims.[7]

In April 2002, the International Chamber of Commerce (ICC) conducted a poll of 1,000 economists and business experts worldwide to gain information on how the world economy was recovering from the terrorist attacks of September 11. Respondents were asked to assess their own country's prospects on a quarterly basis, taking account of trade figures, inflation and interest rate expectations, investment climate, and other key economic indicators.[8]

The results of the 2003 poll reached an all time low in October 2001, immediately following the terrorist attacks on the United States. However, by January 2002 the results had reached the level of July 2001, signaling at least some redemption after the attacks. ICC's Director of Business Surveys, Dr. Gernot Nerb, commented:

> Our experience is that three consecutive positive survey results will be needed before we can be sure that we are looking at the onset of a worldwide recovery. The April and July surveys with ICC will be crucial for predicting the timing and strength of the recovery.[9]

The results of the 2003 poll were published May 15, 2002. "A sharp rise in the ICC world economic climate indicator resulted from more optimistic assessments by business executives on every continent for the next six months."[10] The news was received very well. Results were the highest they had been since the end of 2000, which was considered a boom year. Although Dr. Nerb was pleased with the results, he warned, "The July survey will be crucial in determining the strength and durability of the recovery."[11]

In August 2002, July's results of the quarterly poll conducted by the ICC revealed a slight decline. It had been theorized previously that three polls with improving results would indicate an overall speedy recovery globally from the devastating terrorist attacks of 2001. Dr. Nerb commented, "Business nerves are holding up remarkably well, and this has to be a positive sign for the economic outlook."[12] It is theorized that the recovery did not happen as quickly as the world would have liked.

In May 2002, Brian Jenkins, a leading authority in international security, advised all companies that they should increase the amount of money they spend in protection and safety to counteract the disruption that is caused by terrorist acts. Mr. Jenkins is the advisor to several major corporations worldwide. He made these comments in Denver at the World Congress, International Chamber of Congress. "Capture the lessons learned before memories dim and mythology sets in. This should be a priority," said Mr. Jenkins. Earlier in the year, Mr. Jenkins testified before a congressional hearing on commercial crime "that one estimate put economic disruption in the aftermath of 11 September at $3 trillion." He also testified that the biggest threats or disruptions were in the travel and transportation sectors of international business. He feels that security will continue to become a more important part of the company's actions. "How much security is enough? What is the optimum allocation of security dollars? What is the best combination of risk avoidance, insurance, security, and response preparedness? asked Jenkins.[13]

On October 14-15, 2002, a conference was held in Brussels by the International Chamber of Commerce to look at ways of maximizing trade security while minimizing the impact on international business. The purpose of the symposium is to examine how heightened security measures that have been in place worldwide since September 11, 2001, are affecting world trade. Christopher Harrocks, secretary general of the International Chamber of Shipping, believes that "We are not merely dealing with a threat to trade, but a perceived threat from trade—the bomb in a container, the exploding gas carrier, the anthrax in the consignment."[14]

The 2001 Nobel Prize winner in Economics, Dr. Joseph Stiglitz, a Professor of Economics at Columbia University, took a unique look at the macro-level interconnectivity that can be characterized as "global governance without global government," in which a few institutions, such as the World Bank, the International Monetary Fund, and the World Trade Organization, oversee and dominate financial and commercial interests. His premise is that competitive and social issues pose a significant drawback to the globalization phenomenon. For example, foreign investment, which has had an incredible impact on the growth of foreign markets, such as China, has a downside when it destroys local competitors hoping to develop local industry. This has been seen where Coke and Pepsi have overwhelmed foreign soft-drink manufacturers in their own markets. Global health issues, such as the spread of AIDS, pose enormous health challenges that go beyond the capability of the World Health Organization. Dr. Stiglitz points out that globalization increases the interdependence of the world's population. The need for global collective action has augmented, yet is severely inadequate. The world since September 11, 2001, is continually more complex, and collective action at any level is tough. Stiglitz feels that despite emerging markets with lucrative potential global opportunities, such as China, Korea, eastern Europe, and Georgia, millions of people actually have been made worse off as they have seen their jobs destroyed and lives more insecure and powerless.[13]

CONCLUSION

The international global community has come a long way since September 11, 2001. In October 2001, as the loss of life was still being calculated the economic downturn that started at 8:45 a.m. on September 11, 2001, had hit rock bottom. The outlook was bleak. Today the United States stands strong, an active participant in the global financial world. The world stands by the United States ready to aid, in the realization that their economic success relies very heavily on the most powerful country in the world.

As conditions globally continue to improve the threat of terrorism is still very real. Stated earlier economic conditions have been steadily improving globally since October 2001. There is no way to go from the bottom but up. International business continues to thrive with the knowledge that the only way to truly stand up to terrorism as a corporation is to have crisis teams in place to deal with the disruption that terrorism is bound to cause when it strikes. As governments spend money internally to defend themselves and eradicate the threat of terrorism, so too should businesses dealing in the global economy.

As the markets of the globe begin and continue to recover, it is up to the governments and corporations of each country to strive toward the ultimate goal of financial success. In unsure times, a strong economy is a good thing. When terrorists attack Washington or New York, bomb nightclubs in Bali, and attempt to hijack Israeli planes, they are not assaulting an individual nationality. They are assaulting the citizens of the world.

In the face of despair, when the ashes of the World Trade Center were still smoldering and the world, especially the United States had a collective face of absolute shock and inconsolable grief, business continued. Life continued even though it had been so severely altered. As a nation and a global community it was obvious that to fight terrorism, to discourage terrorism, and to defeat terrorism, life must continue. Not "business as usual," but rather, "business despite what happened."

Has the impact of September 11, 2001, led to "many thin companies"? The answer is yes, considering what has happened to organizations and industries. This "thinning" suggests the need for certain workforce skills to effectively work in this intensely volatile, competitive business environment. The post–September 11 environment warrants the ability for managers, employees, and salespeople to handle complexity and problem solving, effectively communicate ideas, initiate fast decisions, and possess industry expertise. A new capable workforce has evolved, out of urgency, from more streamlined organizations with fewer employees expected to do more work than ever before. This is characterized by greater productivity and performance in less time, responding to urgent work demands, greater customer responsiveness, better time and resource management, and the need for improved innovations and more core competencies. The most critical strategic ability for organizations, in the aftermath of September 11, 2001, is an understanding of their customer's needs to meet the challenge of customer retention and developing crisis management and planning for unpredictable events.[16]

Notes

Chapter 1

1. Tony Carter (2003). September 11, 2001 Survey.

2. Llan Cohen, Stephen Fink, Herman Gadon, and Robin Willits (1995). *Effective Behavior in Organizations,* Sixth Edition. Chicago: Irwin.

3. Leslie Kaufman and Leslie Wayne (2001). "Leadership Put to a New Test." *The New York Times,* September 16, p. 1.

4. Ibid.

5. Personal interview, John Myers, Chairman and President, GE Asset Management, March 5, 2003, Staten Island, New York.

6. Julie Flaherty (2000). "For Chiefs in Crisis, It's Survival of the Sorriest." *The New York Times,* September 3, p. 7.

7. Ron Cross and Laurence Pursak (2002). "The People Who Make Organizations Go or Stop." *Harvard Business Review,* 80(6), June, 104-112.

8. Kaufman and Wayne, "Leadership Put to a New Test."

9. Tony Carter (1999). *The Aftermath of Reengineering.* Binghamton, NY: The Haworth Press.

10. Flaherty, "For Chiefs in Crisis."

11. Steven J. Hoch and Howard C. Kunreuther (2001). *Wharton on Making Decisions.* New York: John Wiley and Sons, Inc.

12. Roderick Kramer (2002). "When Paranoia Makes Sense." *Harvard Business Review,* 80(7), July, 62-69.

13. Ronald Heifetz and Marty Linsky (2002). "A Survival Guide for Leaders." *Harvard Business Review,* 80(6), June, 27-39.

14. Karl E. Weick and Kathleen M. Sutcliffe (2000). *Managing the Unexpected.* San Francisco: Josey-Bass.

15. Flaherty, "For Chiefs in Crisis."

16. Ann Papmehl (2002). "Business in an Uncertain World." *CMA Management,* 76(1), 12-15.

17. Rick LaMorte, personal interview.

18. F. Bavaro (2001). "Big Business Pitch in to Help Victims of September 11, 2001." *Business Week,* October 12, 14-16.

19. Tony Carter (1998). *Contemporary Sales Force Management.* Binghamton, NY: The Haworth Press.

20. Ibid.

21. Ibid.

22. Ibid.

23. Ibid.

24. Ibid.

25. Michelle Conlin (2001). "When the Office Is the War Zone." *Business Week,* November 19, 38.

26. Ibid.

27. Kathrene L. Hansen (2002). "Anxiety in the Workplace Post-September 11, 2001 (Beyond the Beltway)." *The Public Manager,* 31(3), 31-36.

28. John Hobel (2001). "All Workplaces Feel the Terror." *Canadian HR Reporter,* October 8, 4.

Chapter 2

1. New York City Independent Budget Office (2002). *Analysis of the Mayor's Preliminary Budget for 2003,* March.

2. The City of New York—Office of Management and Budget (2002). *Financial Plan: Fiscal Years 2002-2003,* February 13.

3. Ibid.

4. Skip Rimer (2002). "Sept. 11 Terror Attacks to Cost U.S. Metros More Than 1.6 Million Jobs in 2002, New Milken Institute Study Shows." *Milken Institute Study,* January 11.

5. Ibid.

6. Fiscal Policy Institute (2001). "Economic Impact on September 11 World Trade Center Attack." September 28.

7. New York City Independent Budget Office, *Analysis.*

8. Rimer, "Sept. 11 Terror Attacks."

9. National Restaurant Association Home Page. 11 April 2002. "Restaurants Respond—Statement on the Impact of Sept. 11 tragedy on the Nation's Restaurants." November 2002.

10. Rimer, "Sept. 11 Terror Attacks."

11. New York City Independent Budget Office, *Analysis.*

12. Milken Institute Study, 2002.

13. Rimer, "Sept. 11 Terror Attacks."

14. Ibid.

15. National Restaurant Association Home Page. 11 April 2002. "Restaurants Respond—Statement on the Impact of Sept. 11 tragedy on the Nation's Restaurants." November 2002.

16. Jason Bram (1995). "Tourism and New York City's Economy." *Current Issues in Economics and Finance,* 1(7).

17. Bloomberg Preliminary Budget proposal.

18. Tony Carter (1998). *The Aftermath of Reengineering.* Binghamton, NY: The Haworth Press.

19. Christopher Edmonds (2001). "Manhattan Office Space Increases Post Sept. 11." *The Wall Street Journal,* December 14.

20. Bloomberg Preliminary Budget Proposal.

21. Karen Matthews (2002). "Chinatown's Economy Still Suffering After Sept. 11." *New York Newsday*, April 4.

22. Ibid.

23. Jennifer Barrett (2001). "Airlines on the Brink." *Newsweek*, October 17.

Chapter 3

1. Jennifer Barrett (2001). "Airlines on the Brink." *Newsweek*, October 17.

2. Greg Johnson (2001). "After the Attack: Airlines Cautious in Return to Ads: Marketing Campaigns Aim to Restore Confidence Agencies Try to Find the Right Words, Tone to Reach Customers." *Los Angeles Times*, September 24.

3. Stephen Power (2002). "Airlines Improved Quality Measures for Passengers." *Wall Street Journal*, April 9.

4. Air Travel Consumer Report (2001).

5. Sudan Stellin (2001). "Lower Air Fares Through E-Mail." *The New York Times*, December 9.

6. Jennifer Reingold (2001). "Continental's Blunt Leader Faces Crisis, Again." *The New York Times*, September 23.

7. U.S. Department of Transportation (2001). Inspector General's Report.

8. Ibid.

9. Michael McCarthy (2001). "It's time for airline ads on safety, experts say; marketing may take new direction." USA TODAY.com, November 15.

10. Barrett, "Airlines on the Brink."

11. Laurence Zuckerman (2001). "American Airlines Offers Pilots Novel Accord." *The New York Times*, July 25.

12. Shawn Tully (2001). "From Bad to Worse." *Fortune*, October 15, 119-128.

13. Jennifer Barrett. "Airlines on the Brink."

Chapter 4

1. Mike Ahlers (2000). "Report Faults Airline for Communications Gap." *CNN Travel News*, September 27.

2. *National Travel Monitor* (2003).

3. Air Transport Association (1999). "ATA Airlines Announce Customer Service Plan: Carriers to Improve Service with Wide Ranging Proposal." Washington, DC: Air Transport Association.

4. Air Travel Consumer Report (2003).

5. Melinda Bush (2003). "Travelers Future Changes." *Hotel and Motel Management Magazine*, November 3.

6. American Express Corporation (2002). "American Express Leisure Travel Index." June 5. New York: American Express.

7. "Airlines Deliver on Customer Service Commitments: University Report Misleads the Traveling Public and Fails the Fact Test" (2001). Washington, DC: Air Transport Association.

8. American Express Corporation.

9. Laurence Zuckerman (2001). "American Airlines Offers Pilots Novel Accord." *The New York Times*, July 25.

10. Associated Press (2002). "Feds Stand Firm on Bag Screening Deadline." *CNN Travel News*, June 3.

11. Shawn Tully (2001). "From Bad to Worse." *Fortune*, October 15, 119-128.

12. "Summer Travel: Wheels Not Wings." *CNN Travel News*, May 30, 2002.

13. "Consumer Airline Complaints Doubled in '99." *Washington Post*, February 3, 1999

14. "Carriers Retract $20 Fare Hike." *The New York Times*, June 3, 2002.

15. "Summer Travel: Wheels Not Wings." *CNN Travel News*, May 30, 2002.

16. Ibid.

17. Josh Friedman, Bart Lazar, and Robert Mignin (2002). "Privacy Issues in the Workplace: A Post September 11 Perspective." *Employee Relations Law Journal*, 28(1), Fall, 7-24.

18. "Consumer Airline Complaints Doubled in '99." *Washington Post*, February 3, 1999.

19. Boeing Corporation (2001). "Boeing/Wirthlin Worldwide Survey." September-October 2001. Seattle: Boeing, October.

20. Richard Oliver (1997). *Satisfaction.* Boston: Irwin-McGraw Hill.

Chapter 5

1. Air Transportation of America Report (2003).

2. Air Transport Association of America, Inc. (2001). "Airline Economic Impact." October 24.

3. Air Transportation of America Report.

4. Pam Belluck and Laurence Zuckerman (2001). "An Early Economic Fallout, Major Carriers Cut Back." *The New York Times*, September 17.

5. L. Keith Alexander (2002). "The Price Is Different." *Washington Post*, April 6.

6. Katrina Brooker and Alynda Wheat (2001). "The Chairman of the Board Looks Back." *Fortune*, May 28, 63-76.

7. Marilyn Adams (2002). "Hotels, Airline Spend Big, Lure Travelers Back." *USA Today*, March 14.

8. Sherri Day (2001). "Delta Announces Job Cuts and Reductions in Service." *The New York Times*, September 27.

9. Pam Belluck and Laurence Zuckerman (2001). "An Early Fallout, Major Carriers Cut Back." *The New York Times*, September 17.

10. Heide Shrager (2004). "The Fractured Families of 9/11." *Staten Island Advance*, February 22, A1, A7.

11. David Goetzl (2002). "2002 Lookout: Travel." *Advertising Age*, January 7.

12. Brad Foss (2001). "United Airlines' Frank Ads Get Mixed Reviews." *Los Angeles Times*, October 22.

13. Nancy Fonti (2001). "Travel Insider; High-Tech Messaging Smoothes the Flight Path." *Los Angeles Times*, December 16.

14. Steven Greenhouse (2001). "Northwest and American to Pay Severance Benefits." *Los Angeles Times,* September 29.

15. M. Laura Holson and Laurence Zuckerman (2001). "Boeing and United Plan to Lay Off Thousands." *The New York Times,* September 19.

Chapter 6

1. John Sherry (1995). *Contemporary Marketing and Consumer Behavior.* Thousand Oaks, CA: Sage.

2. Ann Marie Kerwin (2001). "Newspapers and Newsweeklies React to NYC Attack." *Advertising Age,* September 17.

3. Lisa Sanders (2001). "Marketers Rally Round the Flag." *Advertising Age,* September 24.

4. Lisa Sanders (2001). "Agencies Study Wartime America." *Advertising Age,* November 26.

5. Lisa Sanders (2001). "Agencies Study Wartime America." *Advertising Age,* November 26.

6. Hoag Levins (2002). "Public's Mood and Confidence on Upswing." *Advertising Age,* January 2.

7. Tony Carter (2003). "September 11, 2001 Survey."

8. Hoag Levins (2002). "Market Shift in New Years Resolutions." *Advertising Age,* January 3.

9. Dan Lippe (2002). "Taste for Luxury Survives Attacks." *Advertising Age,* March 11.

10. Hillary Chiura (2002). "America Concerned but Not Cowed." *Advertising Age,* March 11.

11. Rance Crain (2002). "Advertising Alone Won't Boost Economy." *Advertising Age,* April 22.

12. Carrie Rentschler, Carol Stabile, and Jonathan Sterne (2002). "Mood of the Market: Consumer Behavior in Wartime America." *Advertising Age,* May.

13. Carrie Rentschler, Carol Stabile, and Jonathan Sterne (2002). "United We Stand—Fresh Hoagies Daily." *Bad Subjects,* February.

14. Richard Oliver (1997). *Satisfaction.* Boston: Irwin-McGraw Hill.

15. Marc Gunther (2001). "Ad Libbing." *Fortune,* October 29.

Chapter 7

1. Leslie Kaufman and Leslie Wayne (2001). "Leadership Put to a New Test." *The New York Times,* September 16, p. 1.

2. Julie Flaherty (2000). "For Chiefs in Crisis, It's Survival of the Sorriest." *The New York Times,* September 3, p. 7.

3. W. Chankim and Renee Mauborgne (2002). "Charting Your Company's Future." *Harvard Business Review,* 80(6), June, 76-83.

4. Lee, 2001.

5. Roderick Kramer (2002). "When Paranoia Makes Sense." *Harvard Business Review*, 80(7), July, 62-69.

6. Ronald Heifetz and Donald Caurie (1997). "The Work of Leadership." *Harvard Business Review*, 75(1), January-February, 124-134.

7. Ronald Heifetz and Marty Linsky (2002). "A Survival Guide for Leaders." *Harvard Business Review*, 80(6), June, 27-39.

8. F. Bavaro (2001). "Business Pitch In To Help Victims of September 11, 2001." *Business Week*, October 12, 14-16.

9. E. Illeroif (2002). "Corporations Search Internet for New Markets." *The Wall Street Journal*, March 4, p. 2.

10. Maher, 2001.

Chapter 8

1. Aon Corporate Communications (2001). "Aon Reports Third Quarter 2001 Earnings; Updates on Business transformation, Impact of September 11 Attacks and Spin-offs Plans." November 7.

2. Jessica Papin (2001). *Because We Are Americans: What We Discovered on Sept. 11, 2001.* Warner Books.

3. Tony Carter (1999). *The Aftermath of Reengineering.* Binghamton, NY: The Haworth Press.

4. Jack Gibson (2001). "Attack on America: Insurance Coverage Issues." International Risk Management Institute Inc., September.

5. Lingling Wei (2002). "Giuliani teams up with Aon to provide Crisis Management." *SmartMoney*, October 16.

6. Aon Corporate Communications (2001). "Aon Provides Update on World Trade Center Tragedy." September 12.

7. Tony Carter (1998). *Contemporary Sales Force Management.* Binghamton, NY: The Haworth Press.

8. Stephen Labaton (2002). "Threats and Responses: The Insurance Industry's Tentative Deal Is Reported on $100 Billion in Aid to Insurers Facing Terror Claims." *The New York Times*, October 18.

9. Aon Corporate Communications (2002). "An Insurance Market Overview." November 1.

10. Labaton, "Threats and Responses."

11. Joseph Treaster (2002). "Threats and Responses: The Insurers: Aon Is Moving to New Offices, but Will Avoid Tall Buildings." *The New York Times*, September 10.

12. Fiscal Policy Institute (2001). "Economic Impact of September 11 World Trade Center Attack." September 28.

13. Lingling Wei (2002). "Giuliani teams up with Aon to provide Crisis Management." *SmartMoney*, October 16.

14. Aon Corporate Communications (2001). "Aon Provides Update on World Trade Center Tragedy." September 12.

Chapter 9

1. Personal Interview, George King, 20-20 Advisors, New York, New York, April 15, 2003.

2. Harishsujan (1999). "Extending the Learned Helplessness Paradigm: A Critique of Schulman's 'Learned' Optimism." *Journal of Personal Selling and Sales Management,* 19(1), Winter, 39-49.

3. Harishsujan, "Extending the Learned Helplessness Paradigm."

4. Josh Friedman, Bart Lazar, and Robert Mignin (2002). "Privacy Issues in the Workplace: A Post September 11 Perspective." *Employee Relations Law Journal,* 28(1), Fall, 7-24.

5. Friedman, Lazar, and Mignin, "Privacy Issues in the Workplace."

6. Barbara Bartlein (2003). "September 11, 2001, Slow Economy Changes Employee Priorities." *The Business Journal of Jacksonville,* May 5.

7. Friedman, Lazar, and Mignin, "Privacy Issues in the Workplace."

8. Rita Frankenberry (2002). "Fighting Cybercrime, Despite New Laws Computer Viruses On The Rise." *Inside Business: The Hampton Roads Business Journal,* 22, September; T. Gattipaldi (2002). "Total Manpower Hours Lost As a Result of September 11, 2001." *Labor News,* March, 12.

9. Avaya press release, October 24, 2001.

10. Personal Interview, Robert Marano, PriceWaterhouseCoopers, New York, New York, April, 15, 2003.

11. Gattipaldi, "Total Manpower Hours Lost."

12. M.C. Langfelder and D. Perez (2002). "New Ways to Target Your Market." *Chilton Insights,* April, 14.

Chapter 10

1. Joseph E. Stiglitz (2002). *Globalization and Its Discontents.* New York: W. W. Norton.

2. Cateora and Graham. *International Marketing.*

3. Ibid., p. 5.

4. Ibid., p. 1.

5. Tony Carter (2003). *Customer Advisory Boards.* Binghamton, NY: The Haworth Press.

6. Maria Livanos Cattaui (2001). "What Business Should Do to Thwart the Terrorists." *Business Week,* September 18, p. 12.

7. Ibid.

8. Eileen McMorrow (2002). "The Top Security Threats." *Facilities Design and Management,* November-December, p. 6.

9. Kathrene L. Hansen (2002). "Anxiety in the Workplace Post-September 11, 2001 (Beyond the Beltway)." *The Public Manager,* 31(3), 31-36.

10. Ann Papmehl (2002). "Business in an Uncertain World." *CMA Management* 76(1), 12-15.

11. Kathrene L. Hansen (2002). "Anxiety in the Workplace Post-September 11, 2001 (Beyond the Beltway)." *The Public Manager,* 31(3), 31-36.

12. Papmehl, "Business in an Uncertain World."

13. Eileen McMorrow (2002). "The Top Security Threats." *Facilities Design and Management,* November-December, p. 6.

14. Paul Bluestein (2002). "One Year Aftermath of the Attacks." *The Washington Post,* September 10, p. E1.

15. Personal Interview, Dr. Joseph Stiglitz, Columbia University, New York, New York, October 28, 2002.

16. Tony Carter (2003). September 11, 2001, Survey.

Index

Order a copy of this book with this form or online at:
http://www.haworthpress.com/store/product.asp?sku=5310

MANY THIN COMPANIES
The Change in Customer Dealings and Managers Since September 11, 2001

_____ in hardbound at $39.95 (ISBN: 0-7890-2247-8)

_____ in softbound at $22.95 (ISBN: 0-7890-2248-6)

Or order online and use special offer code HEC25 in the shopping cart.

COST OF BOOKS_____

POSTAGE & HANDLING_____
(US: $4.00 for first book & $1.50
for each additional book)
(Outside US: $5.00 for first book
& $2.00 for each additional book)

SUBTOTAL_____

IN CANADA: ADD 7% GST_____

STATE TAX_____
(NY, OH, MN, CA, IL, IN, & SD residents,
add appropriate local sales tax)

FINAL TOTAL_____
(If paying in Canadian funds,
convert using the current
exchange rate, UNESCO
coupons welcome)

☐ **BILL ME LATER:** (Bill-me option is good on
US/Canada/Mexico orders only; not good to
jobbers, wholesalers, or subscription agencies.)

☐ Check here if billing address is different from
shipping address and attach purchase order and
billing address information.

Signature_____

☐ **PAYMENT ENCLOSED: $**_____

☐ **PLEASE CHARGE TO MY CREDIT CARD.**

☐ Visa ☐ MasterCard ☐ AmEx ☐ Discover
☐ Diner's Club ☐ Eurocard ☐ JCB

Account # _____

Exp. Date_____

Signature_____

Prices in US dollars and subject to change without notice.

NAME_____

INSTITUTION_____

ADDRESS_____

CITY_____

STATE/ZIP_____

COUNTRY_____ COUNTY (NY residents only)_____

TEL_____ FAX_____

E-MAIL_____

May we use your e-mail address for confirmations and other types of information? ☐ Yes ☐ No
We appreciate receiving your e-mail address and fax number. Haworth would like to e-mail or fax special
discount offers to you, as a preferred customer. **We will never share, rent, or exchange your e-mail address
or fax number.** We regard such actions as an invasion of your privacy.

Order From Your Local Bookstore or Directly From
The Haworth Press, Inc.
10 Alice Street, Binghamton, New York 13904-1580 • USA
TELEPHONE: 1-800-HAWORTH (1-800-429-6784) / Outside US/Canada: (607) 722-5857
FAX: 1-800-895-0582 / Outside US/Canada: (607) 771-0012
E-mailto: orders@haworthpress.com

For orders outside US and Canada, you may wish to order through your local
sales representative, distributor, or bookseller.
For information, see http://haworthpress.com/distributors

(Discounts are available for individual orders in US and Canada only, not booksellers/distributors.)
PLEASE PHOTOCOPY THIS FORM FOR YOUR PERSONAL USE.
http://www.HaworthPress.com   BOF04